TO BE A MUSLIM
ISLAM, PEACE, AND DEMOCRACY

His Royal Highness Prince El Hassan bin Talal

TO BE A MUSLIM
ISLAM, PEACE, AND DEMOCRACY

His Royal Highness
Prince El Hassan bin Talal

In collaboration with Alain Elkann

sussex
ACADEMIC
PRESS

BRIGHTON • PORTLAND

Copyright © Prince El Hassan bin Talal, 2004

The right of Prince El Hassan bin Talal to be identified as author of this work has been asserted in accordance with the Copyright, Designs and Patents Act 1988.

2 4 6 8 10 9 7 5 3 1

First published in 2004 in Great Britain by
SUSSEX ACADEMIC PRESS
PO Box 2950
Brighton BN2 5SP

and in the United States of America by
SUSSEX ACADEMIC PRESS
920 NE 58th Ave   Suite 300
Portland, Oregon 97213-3786

British Library Cataloguing in Publication Data
A CIP catalogue record for this book is available from the British Library.

Library of Congress Cataloging-in-Publication Data
El Hassan bin Talal
   To be a Muslim : Islam, peace, and democracy / Prince El Hassan bin Talal ; in collaboration with Alain Elkann.
      p.   cm.
   Includes bibliographical references and index.
   ISBN 1-903900-81-6 (alk. paper) — ISBN 1-903900-82-4 (pbk.)
 1. Islam. 2. Islam—Universality. 3. Religious pluralism—Islam.
4. Democracy—Religious aspects—Islam. I. Elkann, Alain, 1950– II. Title.

BP161.3 .H373   2004
297.2—dc22

2003017916

The jacket/cover illustration is from *The Art of Calligraphy in the Islamic Heritage*, edited by Dr. Ekmeleddin Ihsanoğlu (Istanbul, 1998; ISBN 92-9063-074-4 [English edition].

The *Frontispiece* of HRH Prince El Hassan bin Talal is courtesy of Photographers Anthony Buckley and Constantine Ltd., London.

Typeset and designed by G&G Editorial, Brighton
Printed by MPG Books Ltd, Bodmin, Cornwall
This book is printed on acid-free paper.

Contents

Foreword

DAVID L. BOREN

His Royal Highness Prince El Hassan bin Talal, in selecting Sussex Academic Press for the publication of this unique book, has given the Press an important opportunity to share with a wider audience the perspectives of one of the strongest proponents of peace and mutual understanding in the Muslim world. Reading and taking into account the information in Prince El Hassan's book is sorely needed in the West in general and in the United States in particular, where there is much ignorance about Islam and where negative opinions of Islam feed on that ignorance. The views and attitudes about Islam in public dialogue since the Osama bin Laden-inspired terrorist attack on the United States on September 11, 2001 require that America's leadership, intellectuals, and the general public inform themselves about Islam.

Americans seek to have a positive input upon the Middle East. The vast majority of our people want to help the people of the Middle East to achieve a better life for themselves and for their children. Above all, the United States seeks to help bring peace to the region and to the world. It is impossible to achieve our own positive goals without understanding the religious beliefs that have such a profound impact upon those in the Islamic world. As one of mankind's three great monotheistic religions, Islam has tremendous influence over a large part of the world's population in a large expanse of the world's territory, as well as over a growing number of Muslims in Europe and America. Islam, in its various interpretations, guides to varying degrees 1.2 billion persons. The American public's and their leaders' views about and understanding of Islam greatly affect United States' relations with Islamic nations and our vital interests: in world politics – as allies, rivals, and foes; economically – as sources of raw materials and goods, and as markets; and, culturally and humanely – as fellow beings from whom we can learn, share, cooperate, and mutually benefit in the quest for better lives for ourselves and our children.

There exist many descriptions of Islam, but the fact that *To Be A Muslim: Islam, Peace, and Democracy* comes from a known person who has global political significance gives it greater credibility. This book is an incisive, personal statement about the essence of Islam by one of the world's leading advocates of inter-faith dialogue and understanding. When I had the privilege of bestowing an honorary doctorate upon Prince El Hassan at a convocation of the University of Oklahoma on April 3, 2002, in conjunction with the University's annual foreign policy conference, the diploma approved by the Board of Regents read:

Doctorate of Humane Letters

His Royal Highness Prince El Hassan bin Talal

Leader in the Cause of Peace and Interfaith Understanding

His Royal Highness, Prince El Hassan bin Talal, has devoted his life to the creation of a society in which pluralism is respected and people of all backgrounds and religions can live and work together in freedom and with dignity. His personal vision, his writings and his leadership for a quarter of a century have greatly impacted interfaith dialogue, commitment to human rights, educational opportunities and the alleviation of poverty.

He has co-chaired the Independent Commission on International Humanitarian Issues. He is currently President of the Club of Rome, Chairman of the Arab Thought Forum, and Moderator of the World Conference on Religion and Peace. He also serves as Chairman of the Policy Advisory Commission for the World Intellectual Property Organization.

His Royal Highness is the author of five books: Palestinian Self-Determination, Search for Peace, A Study on Jerusalem, Christianity in the Arab World *and* To Be a Muslim.

At the University of Oklahoma, he is particularly appreciated for his service as Chair of the Board of Advisors for the University's Center for Peace Studies.

As a man of peace who has fostered mutual understanding among all people by the way in which he has lived his life, the University honors His Royal Highness, Prince El Hassan bin Talal.

This book is another important act in His Royal Highness's life-long efforts to promote inter-faith dialogue, understanding of Islam, world peace, and democratization in the Islamic world. The core of the book is a statement of belief written in a question and answer format that allows Islam's basic tenets to be quickly grasped by a wide audience. In form and content the chapter on what it means to be a Muslim reaches both a Western audience and also Muslims (who themselves can be Westerners) that are seeking to articulate their faith and to explain it to themselves and to others. The questions put by His Royal Highness's collaborator, Alain Elkann, are those very frequently posed by people not knowledgeable about Islam. Prince El Hassan's answers are precise, to the point, and thoroughly informative. His tone is neither apologetic nor assertive but a simple declaration of facts. The Prince's elegant description of the sense of unity of the Muslim community worldwide as well as its concurrent diversity of expression and practice is especially useful for a general audience.

The principal educational value of *To Be A Muslim: Islam, Peace, and Democracy* is that it is aimed at the general public as well as at the small groups of intellectuals and theologians who study faith and religion. This book will hopefully be greatly read and critiqued by scholars and academics. There are classical precedents for such personal statements of Muslim faith. In the past these writings generally took the form of manuals that pilgrims returning from Mecca wrote for the benefit of future travelers. Scholars, as well as non-scholars, also used this framework, and they have been of great value to researchers and students of Islam. The catechism-like format has become increasingly common because it works so well.[1]

---

[1] Muhammad Hamidullah, imam (prayer leader) of the grand mosque in Paris, used the format in his 1960s *Introduction to Islam*, and the *mufti* of the Sultanate of Oman used it in a 1986 booklet, *Who are the Ibadiyya?* published in both Arabic and in English translation.

Preface

by EDWIN G. CORR and ALAIN ELKANN

To Be A Muslim: Islam, Peace, and Democracy is a much needed book at this juncture in history. His Royal Highness Prince El Hassan bin Talal of Jordan uniquely presents the essence of Islam for Westerners – political and governmental leaders, academics, and the general public. His concise and fundamental exposition of Islam will contribute positively and significantly to promoting and sustaining an objective and factual discussion of the relations of Islam and Muslims to the rest of the world community in the twenty-first century. It will help the world's leaders and peoples to define the new security and developmental landscape for progress toward a more peaceful and better world.

In only a few short years the nature of the international system and the verities that shaped the United States and other Western powers' national security interests have undergone fundamental changes. The United States and its allies emerged as victors from the Cold War only to find the world arena crowded with intra-state and ethnic conflicts, rogue states, international criminal networks, and terrorists. A new reality, long under the concealing shadow of the Cold War, surfaced. The United States and its partners have fought in the Balkans, Afghanistan, twice in Iraq, in a number of lesser conflicts, and have declared war on terrorism.

We are in an unfamiliar security environment that must be carefully deciphered. All peace-loving nations have to operate to protect and advance their own national interests, and the peace and development of the world. But identifying and engaging the enemy is perplexing. What should be done is not yet clear. Human and material resources to cope with the terrorist challenges are constrained because of a continuing sluggish world economy. Many countries are currently sorting through the bewildering world disorder in search of a sound strategy and effective courses of action. To take this course it is necessary to better comprehend the world in which we live and act.

Even prior to the terrorist attacks against New York City, Washington D.C., and the airline plane over Pennsylvania on September 11, 2001, the West had been at war with terrorists, a large percentage of whom originate from Islamic countries (notwithstanding the fact that these terrorists represent only a small percentage of the one billion two hundred million Muslims of the world). These terrorists are inspired by a radical interpretation of Islam to carry out military *jihad* against the West. In the war on terrorism, the United States and its allies invaded Afghanistan to topple the Taliban and they continue a military campaign to capture Osama bin Laden and to crush al-Qaeda. The United States invaded and now occupies militarily Iraq where much of the resistance persists in the name of Islam.

President David L. Boren notes in his 'Islamic Societies' that there is much ignorance about Islam in the West, and that negative opinions of Islam feed on that ignorance. Knowledge and understanding of those perceived as one's rivals, adversaries, and foes – of those with whom one is in contention and by whom one feels threatened – does not assure reconciliation or removal of one's fears. However, a basic understanding of and empathy with one's foes are probably essential to move toward a cessation of hostilities, the development of an accord and, hopefully, to constructive and mutually beneficial cooperation.

Prince El Hassan, who is a direct descendant of the Prophet Muhammad, provides in this book the information and insight necessary for such understanding. He gives elegant, simple and, at the same time, erudite answers to the forty-one questions posed by Alain Elkann (who kindly shares the writing of this Preface[2]) and in so doing highlights Islam's fundamental belief structures and humanity. The questions Elkann puts are those frequently asked by people not schooled about Islam. His Royal Highness has dedicated his life to promoting peace and friendship among Muslims, Jews, and Christians.

He has intimate knowledge of the Qur'an, is well versed in the Torah and the Bible, and has dialogued with the world's religious, intellectual, political, business, and governmental leaders. In this book he reveals a moderate and clear picture of Muslims, their religion and their history. For Prince Hassan, the main body of Islam should not be regarded by the West as hostile but as part of a fraternal world that has common origins with Judaism and Christianity.

To understand the nature and level of terrorism and how it affects the interests of the United States and the West is the duty of responsible governments. The content of this volume is therefore important for policy makers, for it leads toward analysis, reasoned debate, and considered decision making. *To Be A Muslim* offers the opportunity for a more informed dialogue about the sometimes uncomfortable and important subject of Islam and its influence. One of the strengths of democracy is that intelligent and well-meaning men and women can disagree about the nature of appropriate policies and solutions. It helps, however, if protagonists in the

---

2 Edwin G. Corr is Associate Director of the International Programs Center of the University of Oklahoma. He served as the U.S. Ambassador to Peru, Bolivia, and El Salvador, and as Deputy Assistant Secretary of State. He was a Professor of Political Science and is the author and editor of four books and many articles.

Alain Elkann (b. 1950) is a well-known journalist and writer. He is the author of several interviews in book form, such as *Vita di Moravia/A Life of Moravia* (Bompiani, 1989), translated into fifteen languages, as well as best-selling novels like *I Tuffo/The Dive* (Mondadori, 1981, republished in 1992 in paperback by Bompiani). He currently lives in Rome and works for Italian Television and the Italian Ministry of Culture.

debate can agree upon an accurate description of the situation and actors. This book does not and is not intended to deal with the correct conduct of the war on terrorism. It does, however, supply basic information and provocative views about a possible future in which the West and the Islamic world can live together harmoniously and cooperatively.

The core of the book is, of course, the Prince's 'To Be A Muslim', preceded by the Prince's *Introduction* – 'Appreciating Other's Traditions and Values' and followed by his 'The Implications of Islam for Civil Society and Democratization' and a *Postscript* – 'Toward a Universal Ethic of Human Understanding'. Two *Afterwords* – 'Islamic Societies and Prospects for Democratization', by former U.S. Senator David L. Boren, and 'A Clash of Civilizations? or Normal Relations with Nations of the Islamic World?' by Ambassador Edward J. Perkins – are designed to frame and enhance Prince El Hassan's presentations on Islam and civic society. *To Be A Muslim* is a revision, update, and expansion of a work previously published by Prince El Hassan and Alain Elkann in Italian, French, and Spanish. 'The Implications of Islam for Civic Society and Democratization' is a revision, update, and expansion of an essay[3] previously published by the Prince.

Edwin G. Corr and Alain Elkann
October 2003

---

3 "Islam and Civil Society" appeared first in *Two Cheers for Secularism*, edited by Sidney Brichto and Richard Harris (UK: Pilkington Press, 1998), chapter 4, pp. 47–53; and was subsequently reprinted in *Continuity, Innovation and Change: Selected Essays* by Majlis El Hassan (Jordan: Amman, 2001), chapter 2, pp. 7–16.

Introduction
Appreciating Others' Traditions and Values

These days it seems as though world history is being determined by exceptions rather than rules. In the wake of the horrific bombings of the World Trade Center and the Pentagon on September 11, 2001, we have all had to re-examine our own values and the values of other cultures. We stand today at the crossroads of our very existence. The choice appears stark: move further away from one another, basing our sense of self and self-interests upon the idea of a threatening 'other'; or move closer together as unique individuals sharing common values that allow us to unite as one human family.

A desire for political power may lead individuals to seek that power through the manipulation of religious beliefs. No culture or religion can claim to have a monopoly on the truth. Yet, to certain people, religion is first and foremost a political means to a personal end, which brooks no diversity or adaptability to new circumstances. Only secondarily – perhaps even incidentally – have extremist beliefs anything to do with the betterment of life for individuals and communities.

World leaders and religious leaders from a number of faiths should be commended for their prompt response in affirming the rights of Sunni and Shi'a Muslim communities to live in peace and work with others to address the common problems facing societies worldwide. In spite of the efforts of these leaders, even some third- and fourth-generation Muslim communities in the West have suffered unjust consequences in the form of a backlash against what is still thought to be a threatening 'other' or a 'fifth column' in society.

In many cases this backlash must be ascribed to ignorance of Islam, as it is expressed in the Holy Qur'an and in the *Ḥadīth* (sayings) and *Sunna* (traditions) of the Prophet Muhammad. The Qur'an enjoins mankind to seek knowledge and to educate children, clearly specifying both boys and girls. It outlines women's rights and minority rights in a way which was unheard of in the Arabian Peninsula (and in most other times and places) before the Prophet's divine revelation. It institutes a public welfare system and exhorts its followers to perform altruistic acts. These are principles to which all civilized communities aspire. Islam does not lay an exclusive claim to them. Clearly, the solution to extremist acts undertaken in the name of a great religion is not to condemn that religion wholesale. Rather, it is to promote on every side its centrist and progressive aspect that will co-exist with diverse cultures and will welcome plurality, but will not tolerate acts of terror and inhumanity.

Islam does not tolerate the irresponsible destructiveness that is terrorism. Such irreligious acts run counter to Islamic practice, as this book will make clear; just as they run counter to the practice of Judaism, Christianity, Buddhism, Hinduism, and indeed all other faiths of mankind. Muslims have been vociferous in their condemnation of terrorism, arguing that terrorist acts violate Islamic law. The Islamic scholar Shaykh Zaki Badawi argues that the atrocities of September 11, 2001 are a violation of Islamic law and ethics. Neither the people who were killed or injured, nor the properties that were destroyed, qualified as legitimate targets in any system of law, especially Islamic law. Sayyed Abdel-Majid al-Khoei has described the attacks as "a criminal and barbaric act removed from every moral code and from every religious and humanitarian principle."

In his farewell sermon, the Prophet Muhammad, addressing the thousands of pilgrims at the foot of the Mount of Mercy, said: "God has made inviolable for you each other's blood and each other's property until you meet your Lord." He was reminding them of the Qur'anic decree that to destroy the life of one individual amounts to destroying the entire human race (5:32).[4] The Qur'an emphasizes that those who disturb the peace of society and spread fear and disorder deserve the severest punishment that can be imposed (5:33).

No school of Islam allows the targeting of civilians. An insurrectionist who kills non-combatants is guilty of *baghi* (armed transgression) – a capital offense in Islamic Law. Those who commit such atrocities and claim to do so in the name of, and using the sacred symbols of, any religion are the enemies of us all – indeed, they are the enemy within. Such people do nothing for religion. On the contrary, they have taken up arms against true people of faith. By wrongly ascribing the name of Islam to their perpetration of such a horrendous crime, the September 11 terrorists have propagated a lie that wanton violence plays a role in Muslim belief or activity. This lie can only be swallowed by onlookers who mistake politics for faith and a narrow nihilist outlook for religious fervor.

Every society today recognizes certain ancient traditions of good human behavior: respect for life, justice, altruism, trustworthiness, dignity and understanding. These values need to be enacted by each citizen within a stable civil society. Civil society represents two ideals: first, the right of each citizen to interact with a representative and accountable government; and, secondly, the maintenance of a code of behavior that can guide interactions between civil society and the state as well as within civil society itself. The chapter 'The Implications of Islam for Civil Society and

---

4 In the Qur'an, the first number refers to the chapters (*suras*), and the second to verses.

Democratization' discusses in more detail such interactions in the Muslim world.

Still, Muslim society today has to strive to live up to the precepts of Islamic doctrine. This effort can only take place in the context of basic human rights and education – including education in Islam itself. The exacerbation of poverty, illiteracy, and despair inevitably produces people who will contemplate terrible acts in a last-ditch attempt to survive. If those who are in a position to help respond with disinterest or, even worse, with double standards toward the plight of endangered populations in the developing world, they will only increase the appeal and potency that local extremist approaches can command.

In a moral crisis of these dimensions, we draw strength from the clear ethical standards that have been set throughout time – the examples of justice, compassion, generosity, and imagination that we ascribe to our great founders of civilization. They provide a standard by which we may determine our own civilized responses; and a viable response by civilization to any challenge, not only the problem of terrorism, must be just that – civilized. Right intentions cannot prevail when the wrong means are employed. Choosing the right means is essential during a crisis so that its aftermath can be properly and humanely dealt with, so that those involved can share necessary information and ideas at all levels, and so that human security for each individual – including the 'soft security' of human dignity and cultural rights – can be better ensured for the future. Our present anxieties compel us to determine who our allies are all over the world in the common struggle to resolve global issues through moderate and progressive agendas.

There has been much talk of promoting 'moderate' Muslim belief. 'Moderate' is an ambiguous term. It hardly seems appropriate at this time to contemplate a wavering or uncertain approach in promoting centrist Islamic principles – such as human dignity, respect for life, justice, and

4

generosity – as part of a wider humanitarian effort. On the contrary, such a humanitarian effort must be undertaken with vigor and certainty. We do not strive for just a moderate belief in human rights or a moderate desire for peace.

At the international level there is some hope that, by conversing cultural and social barriers, we may recognize, once and for all, the values to which we all subscribe and which should form the foundation stones of a universal code of conduct. Part of any global response is therefore for us all to become better informed about each other. Effective education is the key to comprehension; comprehension, as we say in Arabic, precedes understanding. It is the understanding of each other's similarities and, just as important, of each other's differences, that we need in order to move forward together.

In this context it becomes necessary to think in terms of a 'Parliament of Cultures', as proposed by the late Yehudi Menuhin, which could provide a framework for dialogue and cooperation between different traditions. This would involve intra-regional efforts toward conversation. It would also be a starting point for dialogue between regions worldwide. It would support bridge-building between whole cultures, because it would provide a way to locate and emphasize the values, purposes, and visions that all civilizations share and will continue to share.

In the years ahead, as the horrific images of devastation now etched in our memories continue to haunt us, we will look for ways to reinforce our common humanity and identify our common fears. For make no mistake: the attacks of September 11, 2001 were aimed at one civilization composed of many nations and not at one nation alone. The global transition from a culture of violence to a culture of peace is our major challenge. We must learn to live together, demonstrate solidarity, share knowledge and experience, and practice the appreciation of others' traditions and values. As ibn 'Arabi, the thirteenth-century Sufi traveler and mystic, phrased his vision of the pluralist approach:

> *My heart is open to all the winds:*
> *It is a pasture for gazelles,*
> *And a home for Christian monks;*
> *A temple for idols,*
> *The Black Stone of the Mecca pilgrim,*
> *The table of the Torah,*
> *And the book of the Qur'an.*
> *Mine is the religion of love.*
> *Wherever God's caravans turn,*
> *The religion of love*
> *Shall be my religion*
> *And my faith.*[5]

An important step toward our acceptance of one another is to act positively concerning our values – by confessing to each other what we believe to be true and good. This frank expression of belief, and willingness to reach out, is as necessary within the many schools and sects of Islam as it is between Islam and other faiths. Hence the publication of this book.

---

5 Ibn 'Arabi, tr. from *Tarjuman al-Ashwaq*; also tr. as no. XI in *The Tarjuman al-Ashwaq: a Collection of Mystical Odes*, by Muhyiddin ibn al-'Arabi, translated by R. A. Nicholson (London, 1911; repr. 1978), pp. 66–67.

To Be A Muslim

1 What does it mean to be a Muslim?

To be a Muslim means to recognize the existence of the one and only true God: the invisible yet omnipotent, omnipresent and omniscient creator of the world, who has entrusted the world to mankind to manage in accordance with the divine moral imperative as revealed through a succession of prophets, or messengers of God.

It means to acknowledge Muhammad as the last prophet to whom the divine imperative was revealed in the Qur'an, in its original, unadulterated, and most authoritative form. Muslims see themselves as being part of the long tradition of submission to the will of God, which had been the essence of monotheistic religions from the beginning of the world. They do their best to live according to the divine imperative, to promote the good and to combat evil in this world. They believe that they are individually and collectively accountable in the hereafter – not only for their deeds, but also for their intentions.

2 How do you feel to be a direct descendant of the Prophet Muhammad, and what kind of responsibility is it for you?

Islam holds all the faithful to be potentially equals, regardless of origin or lineage, maintaining that the nearest of them to God are those that do most good to mankind. Accordingly, being a direct descendant of the Prophet Muhammad does not in itself make one Muslim better than another. Historically, however, descendants of the Prophet, as Muslims, have felt it incumbent upon them in a special way to serve their community, guard its interests, and act responsibly on its behalf. Among Muslims, moreover, the historical norm has been to turn to members of *Al al-Bayt* (the Prophet's family) for leadership or counsel in times of trouble or distress, or whenever they found their ranks divided. As a member of *Al al-Bayt*, I do not hold myself to be necessarily a better Muslim than others; yet I do consider myself especially called on to guard what I interpret to be the best interests of my fellow Muslims, and to promote their standing in the modern world within the framework of the interests of humanity at large, with prejudice to none.

3 How many Muslims are there in the world?

According to the most recent estimates, all denominations included, Muslims rank, next to Christians, as the second largest religious community in the world. Numerically, Christians of the world were last estimated at about 2 billion, while Muslims are estimated at about 1.2 billion. Proportionately, Christians are estimated at 40.8 percent of the world population; while Muslims are estimated at 23.5 percent.

4 Was Muhammad a prophet like Moses or Jesus?

Following the teaching of the Qur'an, Muslims honor Moses and Jesus, holding them to be prophets of the same ranking as Muhammad and entitled to equal reverence. The same word of God was revealed to all three: to Moses, as the Torah; to Jesus, as the Gospel; to Muhammad, as the Qur'an. The Qu'ran says: ❴❂❵ The messenger believes in that which has been revealed unto him from his Lord and (so do) believers. Each one believes in Allah and His angels and His scriptures and His messengers – We make no distinction between any of His messengers – and they say:

"We hear, and we obey. (Grant us) Thy forgiveness, our Lord. Unto Thee is the journeying." ❀❀ (2:285).[6] The message brought by all the prophets, according to the Qur'an, was the same: to believe in the One God and obey Him. The Prophet Muhammad is called *khatam al-anbiya'* (the seal of the prophets), confirming and completing that message.

5 What did the Prophet Muhammad preach?

First and foremost, the Prophet Muhammad's own preaching consisted of reciting the words of the Qur'an, as revealed to him by God, making sure these were written down and memorized by others too. He then explained them, both in his own words and by his own example in his *Sunna* (traditions). All these words were recorded in the *Ḥadīth*. While the Qur'an, for example, enjoins prayer, the *Sunna* sets the pattern for Muslim prayer, as originally performed by the Prophet Muhammad. The Prophet Muhammad preached a system of morals combining mercy and justice, based on belief in the One God, His prophets and scriptures, and the Day of Judgment. It includes regular prayer, charitable giving and other good deeds, fasting at the time of Ramadan, and pilgrimage to Mecca.

6 What is the role of God (Allah) for Muslims?

Allah is the Arabic name for God, used by Jewish and Christian Arabs as well as by Muslims. It is not the name of Islam's special God. There is actually no other name for God in the Arabic language, barring the divine epithet *al-Rabb* (the Lord) which is also used by Jewish and Christian

---

6 Quotations from the Qur'an are taken from a number of different sources. A reference that is often used is *The Qur'an*, translated by M. H. Shakir, fourth US edition, 1991, published by Tahrike Tarsile Qur'an, Inc., Elmhurst, New York.

Arabs. Apart from these proper names, there are many attributes known as 'the beautiful names of God'; for example, The Compassionate, The Merciful, The Just, The Peace, and The Almighty.

Islam is no different from Judaism and Christianity in recognizing God as the creator of the world and the ultimate source of its ethical order. The attributes of God are identical in all three religions. Islam, however, rejects the Christian doctrine of the Trinity, regarding this doctrine as being incompatible with the Qur'anic emphasis on the absolute unity of God.

7 What kind of relationship do Muslims have with God, and how do they pray?

Islam does not recognize any intermediary between the human individual and God, such as a church or priesthood. Accordingly, the relationship between the individual Muslim and God is direct. The religious rites enjoined by the Qur'an – such as the five daily prayers, the fast of Ramadan or the pilgrimage – are all performed by personal initiative, starting with the *niyya* (intention). Also, the performance of the individual in any religious rite is regulated entirely by his or her own conscience and individual sense of accountability to God. It is entirely up to the individual Muslim, for example, to make up for a missed prayer, a missed day of fasting, or a failure to pay alms. It is not possible to inculcate religion in people's hearts by force. As it is plainly said in the Qur'an: ❨❂ There is no compulsion in religion❂❩ (2:256). Muslim daily prayer can be performed anywhere: at home, at work, by a roadside, or in a mosque. It may be performed by the individual alone, or in company with others, with one of the group acting as *imam* (prayer leader). Before beginning prayer, Muslims perform ablutions to make them ritually clean, after which they form their intention to pray. To make certain that the ground on which they pray is ritually clean, many Muslims keep a special rug or carpet for the purpose, carrying it with them wherever they go.

The rites of the *salat* (prayer) are performed facing the *qibla* (the direction of Mecca), after which the Muslim may address God directly (the *du'a'*), requesting assistance, forgiveness, or mercy.

In addition to the daily prayers, Muslims are enjoined to take part in the communal prayer held in the mosque at noontime on Fridays: *salat al-Jum'a* (Friday prayer). In principle, the *imam* (leader) who leads this prayer and delivers the Friday oration as the *khatib* (orator) can be any adult male Muslim. The fact that *imams* are appointed for this function gives them no special religious authority; it is merely for the sake of convenience.

8 What does the Qur'an say?

The essentials of the Qur'anic teaching are: (a) that God is one, transcendental, omnipotent, omnipresent, and omniscient; (b) that human beings, individually and collectively, are the stewards/trustees of God on earth, responsible for its good management and the proper use and preservation of all its resources; (c) that all Muslims should live according to God's guidance in the realm of worship, moral conduct, and law; and (d) that human beings, individually and collectively, will be held accountable for all their deeds and intentions on an imminent day of final judgment.

9 Is the Qur'an comparable to the Torah for Jews, and the Gospel for Christians?

Muslims hold the Qur'an to be the eternal and immutable word of God. So, according to Muslim belief, were the Torah and the Gospel as originally revealed to Moses and Jesus, respectively. Muslims believe that the

Qur'an has been preserved intact ever since its first revelation and has maintained its full authority – unlike earlier scriptures, which have not been so well preserved; some of the original teachings in the Torah and the Gospel have been lost or tampered with in one way or another.

10 How do Muslims perceive the other religions?

The Qur'an presents Islam as the original religion recognizing the unity of God. The pre-eminent prophets of Islam, before Muhammad, were Abraham, Moses and Jesus. Thus, to the followers of the Prophet Muhammad, the followers of Moses and Jesus were true Muslims, until they started lapsing into errors, which the Prophet Muhammad was sent to correct – not by compulsion, but by persuasion. Yet the Jews and Christians who persisted in their errors remained *ahl al-kitab* (scriptural peoples) deserving of respect, because they believed in God and the ultimate accountability of mankind before God. So long as they kept their peace with Muslims, Muslims had to keep their peace with them. Those among them who lived among Muslims and respected the Muslim order were entitled not only to full religious and social tolerance but also to protection in case of need. Hence the term *ahl al-dhimma* (communities [committed to the Muslim] conscience), which was historically applied to Jews and Christians in Muslim-dominated lands. In practice, Islamic law extended the same tolerance to all non-Muslim communities under its protection.

11 Is there, for Muslims, a central organization with a supreme authority?

There is no central religious organization in Islam wielding spiritual authority over Muslims. As already pointed out, Islam recognizes no intermediary between the individual Muslim and God.

Traditionally, however, the opinion of *ulama'* (men of religious learning) has commanded special respect in Islam; their pronouncements and rulings on religious and canonical issues, as well as on matters of communal concern, carry special weight. Hence the norm in Muslim states is to entrust the management of religious and judicial institutions to members of the *ulama'* class. Until 1924, the *khalifah* (Caliph) was the head of the largest part of the *Ummah* (community of Islam).

12 Is Mecca the world center for Muslims?

The Qur'an teaches that the Ka'ba, situated almost at the center of the great mosque of Mecca, was the first *bayt* (house) established on earth for the worship of the One God; also, that the Ka'ba was the original *maqam* (shrine) of Abraham (for Muslims, the primeval monotheist) who laid its foundations with the help of his son Ishmael. In keeping with this Qur'anic teaching, Muslims revere the Ka'ba in Mecca as the most holy sanctuary on earth, though not as the geographical center of the world. This is the *qibla* (point) towards which all Muslims face when performing their daily prayers.

13 Why must Muslims make pilgrimage to Mecca?

The Qur'an enjoins pilgrimage to Mecca, to worship at the Ka'ba, at least once in a lifetime for all Muslims capable of undertaking the journey. Accordingly, Muslim jurisprudence recognizes *al-hajj* (pilgrimage) as the fifth of the five *arkan* (pillars) of Islam – the four others being, in order, *shahāda* (profession of the unity of God and the prophethood of Muhammad), *salat* (prayer), *sawm* (Ramadan fast), and *zakat* (almsgiving). Pilgrims go physically to that oldest spot dedicated to the One God, which they face every day in prayer. The pilgrimage is like a great meeting of Muslims from all over the world on equal terms, dressed alike. It also reminds them of the Day of Judgment.

14 What kind of attitude do Muslims have in their way of praying?

When Muslims pray, they stand and bow before God several times a day to acknowledge His greatness above everything. They seek His mercy and affirm their commitment to Him, asking Him for guidance, forgiveness and blessing. This means that they are constantly reminded of their duty to God, which hopefully should improve their behavior toward all His creatures.

15 How many times must Muslims go to the mosque?

The Muslim daily prayers may be performed in the mosque or anywhere else, according to the convenience of the individual. Men are required to perform the Friday communal prayer in the mosque. In many mosques, special areas are reserved for women to partake in the Friday communal prayer, should they so wish.

16 How do Muslims pray?

The Muslim prayer starts with the declaration of the intent to pray. This is done while standing in the upright position. While still standing, the faithful next proclaim the greatness of God with the Arabic statement *Allahu akbar*, (God is most great) after which they recite the *fatiha* (the opening *sura* [chapter] of the Qur'an), followed by the recitation of some Qur'anic verses (a short *sura*, or an excerpt from a larger *sura*), according to the individual's choice. Next, they bow with hands on knees (the *ruku'* position) glorifying God; and, after returning to the upright position, prostrate themselves twice in *sujud* (the prostrate position), again glorifying God. This completes one *rak'a* (prayer cycle), after which they return to the upright position. After the second, they remain seated on their heels, with bent knees, to recite the *tashahhud* (affirmation of faith) asking for peace for the worshippers and all righteous people of God, for the Prophet Muhammad and his family, and for Abraham and his family. Next comes the "salutation": turning the head first to the right, then to the left, Muslims say: *as-salamu alaykum wa rahmatu'llahi wa barakatuh* (Peace be upon you, and the mercy of God, and His blessings). With every change of position, they repeat *Allahu akbar*. The prayer thus starts with declaring the greatness of God and ends with peace for all.

17 The prayers of Islam seem choral. Do you have individual or solitary prayers? Do you have monks in your religion?

The Qur'an may be read or chanted, ordinary chanting being called *tartīl* and elaborate chanting *tajwīd*. The chanting is normally done in communal prayers by the *imam* (leader) only, and may also be done in personal prayers. The prescribed rite of prayer apart, however, Muslims individually are free to communicate with God as they like. And while Islam commends moderate asceticism in day-to-day behavior as a virtue, it does not commend monasticism. Accordingly, there is no such thing as a Muslim monk. In Islam all daily actions, if done properly with the right intentions, can be a worship of God; so a Muslim can be constantly engaged in worship without abandoning the world.

18 Which are the most important religious holidays?

Islam has two annual feasts: the first (duration: three days) marks the end of the Ramadan fast (*'Id al-Fitr* [the feast of the break of the fast] or *al-'Id as-Saghir* [the small feast]). The second (lasting four days) celebrates the end of the pilgrimage: *'Id al-Adha* (the feast of the sacrifice) refers to the sacrifice of sheep in memory of Abraham's submission to God and his willingness to sacrifice his son, which is one of the main pilgrimage rites. It is sometimes called *al-'Id al-Kabir* (the big feast). The ritual for these two feasts involves a special communal prayer, customarily chanted and performed at dawn of the first feast day. Each involves sharing with the poor and visiting others, as well as paying respects at the graves of deceased friends and relatives. In addition, Muslims have come to celebrate the Prophet's birthday, and the Muslim New Year, as well as other occasions marked by the Muslim calendar. For these celebrations, however, there are no set rites, as they are not canonically recognized as feast days.

19 Why do Muslims consider Friday their holy day, like Sunday for Christians and Saturday for Jews?

Friday is the day set by the Prophet Muhammad for the weekly congregational prayer ordained in the Qur'an. Unlike Saturday for Jews and Sunday for Christians, Friday (*al-jum'a* [the coming together]) is not a holy Sabbath day, but the day of the week in which the obligatory communal prayer takes place at midday. Abstaining from work on Friday is not mandatory for Muslims, but simply a convenience. Many Muslims, however, consider it essential to have an adequate noontime break on Fridays to facilitate the performance of the weekly communal prayer. In modern times, Friday has been made an official weekly holiday from work in the majority of Muslim countries; but commercial life and other activities go on as normal.

20 Around the world, many people have a false image of Muslims. They see them as terrorists or 'fundamentalists'.

Terrorism involves the systematic use of acts inspiring terror as a means of political or social coercion, or of attracting public attention to unredressed or unrecognized grievances. The term was first used in the European languages in connection with the stage of the French Revolution known as the Reign of Terror, its first use in English occurring in 1795. It was not until recent decades that it came to have a recognized equivalent in Arabic: *irhab*, from *arhaba* (frightened/intimidated).

One should ask, accordingly, who learned terrorism from whom? Islam, as a religion, does not condone the wanton use of violence, intimidation, or the victimization of the innocent under any condition, and is hence distinctly anti-terrorist in principle. The exercise of terrorism by some claiming to be Muslims in recent decades does not justify the association of terrorism with Islam, any more that the exercise of terrorism in Ireland, for example, justifies the association of terrorism with Roman Catholicism.

Likewise, while the modern world has known Muslim as well as non-Muslim extremists, Islam, in the words of the Qur'an, promotes the management of public affairs through *shura* (dialogue or consultation). This communal governing principle is supported by the fact that the Arabic language has had to borrow the terms *al-fashiyya* (fascism) and *ad-diktaturiyya* (dictatorship) from the European languages, where these terms originated.

21 What do you feel about the fact that some Arab women have their faces covered with veils?

Islam recommends modesty in dress and adornment for women and men – the recommendation coming from the Qur'an, without elaboration or emphasis, in the following words: ❨❀ Tell the believing men to lower their gaze and be modest. That is purer for them. Lo! Allah is aware of what they do. Tell the believing women to lower their gaze and be modest, and to display of their adornment only that which is apparent, and to draw their veils across their bosoms ... ❀❩ (24:30–31).

Christianity makes similar recommendations for women on this matter; the principle of modesty having been made by Saint Paul with considerable elaboration and theological justification: "I want you to understand that the head of every man is Christ, the head of every woman is her husband, and the head of Christ is God. Any man who prays or prophesies with his head covered dishonors his head (meaning Christ); but any woman who prays or prophesies with her head unveiled dishonors her head (meaning her husband) – it is the same if her head were shaven. For if a woman will not veil herself, then she should cut off her hair; but if it is disgraceful for a woman to be shorn or shaven, let her wear a veil. For a man ought not to cover his head, since he is the image and glory of God; but woman is the glory of man. For man was not created from woman; but woman from man. Neither was man created for woman; but woman for man. That is why a woman ought to have a veil on her head ... If anyone is disposed to be contentious [on this matter], we recognize no other practice; nor do the churches of God" (1 Corinthians 11:3–16).[7]

Among Christians the veiling of women ceased to be considered mandatory from an early time, except for nuns – the last vestigial remnant of it for laywomen is the bridal veil. Likewise, many modern Muslims no longer consider veiling mandatory for women. In both cases, this represents a departure from the respective scriptural recommendations. Principally, the difference is that Christian society, particularly in the West, has come to regard the veil as an unacceptable infringement of the right of women to be the social equals of men; while Muslim society, where the veil remains the prevalent tradition, leaves the matter to personal choice. Muslims point out that people in the West no longer condemn nudity and scanty dressing, but now condemn Muslims who choose to cover themselves.

---

7 The Holy Bible, Revised Standard version containing the Old and New Testament, Oxford University Press, London; New Testament section, copyright 1946.

22 Is it true that inside the Muslim world there are many conflicts?

The Qur'an teaches the peaceful resolution of conflicts between Muslims and between others where possible. However, the Muslim world comprises numerous nation-states differing in language, ethnicity, and political orientation; and it is unreasonable to expect these nation-states to be invariably of one heart or mind. Occasionally, clashes of interest between them lead to serious conflicts, sometimes lasting for extended periods. To minimize the possibility of the outbreak of such conflicts, and to attend to other matters of common Islamic interest, Islamic summit meetings are periodically held.

23 Some Muslim countries seem to be ruled by a more strict religious regimen than others. What are the relationships between these countries?

Muslims live in many varied areas of the world. It is not surprising that there are human differences between their numerous countries. Muslim countries, like all others, are strongly averse to infringements of their sovereign prerogatives, even when other Muslim countries in the name of the common religion make these infringements. However, Muslim scholars and writers are under a religious obligation to give sincere advice to other individuals and communities.

24 What kind of relationships are there among Arabs?

Arabs of different countries and regions including immigrants to non-Arab countries have a sense of common peoplehood which they term *al-'Urubah*, (Arabism). This sense of commonality is so deeply ingrained in the Arab soul that it often overrides the existing differences in national affiliation to one country or another. One must not forget that all Arabs speak Arabic, which, in its written form, is one of the oldest languages in the world in continued and uninterrupted use.

Arabic not only provides a fundamental link between Arabs of different countries, but also a link between Arabs of today and the Arabs of past centuries, underpinned by the Muslim/Arab heritage and the cultural ethos of Islam.

While the Arab states' governments often differ in their political agenda and priorities, and are not always of one heart and mind on given issues, the Arab peoples generally are; and Arab states normally take this matter into consideration. The sense of a common Arab cause tends to prevail in inter-Arab politics, particularly in times of crisis.

25 Some Arabs are Muslims and others are Christians. How do they view each other?

Muslim and Christian Arabs share a common linguistic, cultural, and historical heritage, the difference between them being only in religious affiliation. Because of the protection afforded to them by Islam from the beginning (see Qur'an 29:46), Christians have shared with Muslims a common life. The occasional conflicts between them have been rare exceptions to the rule, and are almost always resolved through dialogue. Had this not been the case, Christianity among the Arabs would not have continued to exist until today.

Historically, it was the Christian Arabs, starting from the mid-nineteenth century, who first articulated the concept of *al-'Uruba* (Arabism) as the bond making Christian and Muslim Arabs one people distinct from others. Also, Christian Arabs have featured prominently as intellectual and political leaders of Arab nationalist movements.

26 Which are the basic principles that a Muslim has to follow?

Awareness of God and following His guidance are the fundamental prin-ciples of Islam. God guides people to behave charitably with consideration for others in all walks of life, commanding the faithful to do good and avoid evil; the Muslim distinction between what is good and what is evil being the same as in Christianity. Despite religious differences, Islam and Christianity share the same basic ethical principles. A Muslim's good treatment should be extended to all people and all creatures of God without any distinction. Muslims should cooperate with others in doing what is good and useful to all.

27 What does Ramadan mean, and how do you practice it?

Ramadan is the month of the annual fast, which begins daily at dawn and ends at sunset. All Muslims capable of fasting are expected to do so for the duration of this month.

The first day of the fast normally follows the reported sighting of the new moon of the lunar month, and the last day is determined by the observation of the new moon of *Shawwal* (the month following Ramadan). While some Muslims today recommend that the start and the end of the Ramadan fast be established astronomically rather than by reported sighting, the idea has not yet gained general acceptance.

Every day, Muslims begin their fast after *as-suhur* (a special pre-dawn meal) by affirming the intention to fast, after which they abstain from taking any food or drink or from smoking or sexual activity until the *maghrib* (sunset) call to prayer, when the daily fast is broken by a meal called *iftar* (breakfast). (The fast by day is interpreted to include absten-tion from taking any medications, orally or by injection.) Missed days of fasting, because of temporary illness, travel, or any other reason, should be made up for subsequently at the individual's discretion and convenience. While fasting, the faithful are enjoined to think of the poor and perform acts of charity. If unable to fast for any permanent reason, the Qur'an enjoins Muslims to feed a poor person for each day missed. The nights of Ramadan, between *iftar* and *suhur*, bring families and friends together, and involve social gatherings which vary with the local culture.

The fast apart, Ramadan is regarded in Islam as a month of particular holiness because it was the one in which the Prophet Muhammad received his first Qur'anic revelation. In the Qur'an, Muslims are urged to fast ❲❁ that you may attain God-consciousness ❁❳ (2:183). Fasting therefore entails spiritual recharging, additional prayers, recitation of the Qur'an, meditation, and restraining bad behavior. The Prophet said: "If you do not refrain from bad language and bad actions, God has no need of your refraining from food or drink (ḥadīth)."[8]

28 Why, in Muslim countries and communities, does one hear the muezzin calling for prayer at certain times of the day?

The *adhān* (call to prayer) was instituted by the Prophet Muhammad to replace the *shopher* (trumpet) used by Jews and the *naqus* (bell) used by Christians, for the same purpose. It announces the start of the due time for each of the five daily prayers, calling local people to attend the mosque if they can. In the *adhān*, the muezzin (*mu'adhdhin*) – the caller to prayer – makes the following call:

> *Allahu akbar* ("God is most great," repeated twice).
> *Ashhadu anna la ilaha illa-Llah* ("I testify that there is no deity other than God," repeated twice).

---

8 Muhammad Nasser ed-din Al-Albani, *Saḥīḥu Sunani ibni Majah* [in Arabic] (Beirut: Islamic Bureau, 1986), Vol. I, ḥadīth No. 1370, p. 282.

Ashhadu anna Mumammadan rasulu-Llah ("I testify that
Muhammad is the prophet of God," repeated twice).

Hayya 'ala's-salat ("come to prayer," repeated twice).

Hayya 'ala'l-falah ("come to salvation/success," repeated twice).

Allahu akbar ("God is most great," repeated twice).

La ilaha illa-Llah ("there is no deity other than God," said only
once).

Subsequent tradition supplemented the *adhān* with blessings upon the
Prophet Muhammad, his family, and his companions.

Apart from the practice in some of the stricter Muslim rites, the
adhān is normally chanted and even sung in varying melodies. In some
Muslim countries, the singing of the *adhān*, like the chanting of the
Qur'an, is a highly developed art. In modern times loudspeakers are used
and the *adhān* is also called on TV channels and the radio.

As the *adhān* is an Islamic practice, it is not restricted to Arab countries, but can be heard wherever Muslims are allowed to announce their
prayers publicly.

29 How does one behave in a mosque?

To Muslims the mosque is primarily a place for individual or communal
worship, though it also serves as a place for rest and private contemplation, and a forum for meeting, religious instruction, and the discussion of
public affairs. As a place where people prostrate themselves to the ground
in prayer, its floor – normally covered with mats, rugs, or carpets – is
supposed to remain ritually clean. Accordingly, Muslims should enter the
mosque without shoes, or wear special slippers or shoes that are kept
clean. Inside the mosque, they are expected to behave and dress with
decorum, much as Christians are expected to behave in a church, and

cause no disturbance to people who happen to be praying. They may walk about freely, sit on the floor, or engage quietly in conversation – the atmosphere of the mosque, except for the time of communal prayers, being informal. There is no rule that prevents non-Muslims from entering mosques; mosques of special historical, archaeological, or architectural standing actually attract many non-Muslim visitors. Muslims engaging in individual or communal prayer, however, are naturally averse to being disturbed or viewed as objects of curiosity by such visitors.

30 Are men and women separated in mosques?

Mosques are open to women as well as to men; but women and men perform communal worship in the mosque separately, albeit following the same *imam* (prayer leader). In some mosques (normally the larger ones), special areas are set aside to make it possible for women to participate in communal worship. The *salat* (prayer) involves standing close together, leaving no gaps in the line; it also involves kneeling, sitting close together, and prostrating. So it is considered more proper and comfortable for the sexes to be separated.

31 What is the role of men? What is the role of women?

Islam accords men and women equal standing as believers. This is implicit in the Qur'an, which addresses itself to men and women jointly. In Islam, however, as in Judaism and Christianity, the man, as husband or father, is regarded as the legitimate head of the family, provided he behaves responsibly and in accordance with the *shari'a* (Muslim law). This does not give him rights over property which his wife or wives may hold independently from him. Such property is the wife's to manage at her own discretion. A Muslim woman enjoys Qur'anically specified rights of inheritance from her father, mother, husband, and/or sons and other relatives. Furthermore, the advance of money paid by the bridegroom to the bride when the contract of marriage is concluded between them automatically becomes part of the wife's independent property, as does the delayed bride-gift specified for the wife by the marriage contract, which she receives in case of divorce. The husband has to shoulder all the financial responsibility for the family. Both should cooperate in household work, as the Prophet did.

32 Why can a Muslim man have four wives at the same time?

The norm in Islam is monogamy, but Islam recognizes that there are some circumstances when the need arises for polygamy: for example, in war when men are in short supply, or when the wife is unable to bear children and her husband would otherwise have to divorce her before marrying again. Allowing polygamy also provides an opportunity for recognition of all of a man's wives and children and ensures his responsibility to provide for them all, as well as their right to inherit from him. The Qur'an permits the marriage of a man to as many as four wives at the same time, provided he can maintain all his wives and accord them equal treatment; otherwise it recommends monogamy. In Muslim practice, however, the tendency in modern times has been increasingly toward monogamy.

33 Is divorce accepted in the Muslim religion?

Unlike Christian marriage, Muslim marriage is not a holy sacrament, but a contract between the husband and the wife – much as a civil marriage is, except that the conditions of the contract can vary from one Muslim marriage to the other, both parties having to agree to these conditions. Should a marriage prove unsatisfactory to the husband, he has the right to end it by pronouncing his wife divorced and paying the rest of the bride-gift due to her by the marriage contract. The wife can also take the initiative in divorce provided she had set this condition in the marriage contract, or by getting the husband's agreement. A wife may also seek divorce from an unsatisfactory husband by recourse to Muslim courts of law. In practice, however, the majority of Muslim marriages are normally lasting ones. Although there is no need to go to court, the divorce rate is lower than in many countries that impose lengthy legal procedures.

34 What kind of relationship do Muslims have with their families?

Muslims look after their families much as other people do, caring for their spouses and children as best they can. As a rule, the Muslim family is close-knit; the recognition of the father's authority contributes to keeping it so. Respect for parents is paramount and care for the weaker members is built into the law, forming a social security system with members of the family possessing the right to inherit and receive maintenance from each other as necessary.

35 How does Islam conceive of death?

Islam teaches its followers to accept death gracefully as being ordained by God, and is averse to excessive manifestations of grief. For this reason, Muslim funerals tend to be quiet and dignified. The dead are buried on the day of the death, or the following day, after being washed and dressed in white shrouds. The funeral service immediately precedes the burial. The Muslim dictum has it that the dead are best honored when they are buried; in Arabic, *Ikramu'l-mayti dafnuh.* Death is not the opposite of life, but a further stage on the way to the final return to God. The salutation given to the dead, when visiting graves, is the same as in life; and the dead are spoken to as if they can hear. All will rise on the Day of Resurrection to stand before God for judgment and to account for their deeds.

The funeral prayer, normally in the mosque, is short – containing essential glorification of God, the first *sura* of the Qur'an, blessing of the Prophet, and prayers for the dead and the living. The funeral prayer, procession and burial are open to all, not just the family and invited guests. The body of the dead person is laid in a grave, with the face placed towards the Ka'ba, before being covered with earth. While most Muslim graves are marked with tombstones, moderation is encouraged.

36 For Muslims, is there life after death?

Muslims believe in the immortality of the soul and in the physical resurrection of the body on the *al-Yawm al-Akhir* (Latter Day), or *Yawm ad-Din* (Day of Judgment), when the true believers and the good are rewarded with Paradise, and the disbelievers and the wicked are committed to Hell for as long as God decrees. Belief in life after death and the Day of Judgment are part of the creed of Islam, and Muslims are reminded of this regularly; when ordered to do something or to refrain from doing something, the familiar saying is heard: "if you believe in God and the Day of Judgment." Without accountability there would be no point in asking people to do, or refrain from doing, certain things. In the next life, any injustices that beset this life will be redressed.

37 How do you become Muslim? Does one have to convert by receiving a ritual bath? How is conversion viewed by Muslims?

In principle, a person becomes a Muslim by simply admitting sincere belief in the oneness of God and the prophethood of Muhammad, the formula involved being the Muslim *shahāda*: "I testify that there is no deity other than God; and I testify that Muhammad is the prophet of God."

Although it is recommended for the person to take a ritual bath when becoming a Muslim, Islam prescribes no special conversion rites similar to the Christian sacrament of baptism; nor does it prescribe initiation rites similar to the Jewish *bar mitzvah*, or the Christian confirmation.

(38) Is there racism in the Muslim world?

The Qur'an reminds people that the diversity of races, colors, and languages is a sign of the grace of God, and that ❨❀ the most honored of you in the sight of God is the most righteous❀❩ (49:13). The Prophet had among his closest companions Africans, Persians, and Byzantines. Islam regards all Muslim believers as equals, regardless of race or color. The same is true of Christianity. Individual Muslims may express racist tendencies, but Islam is the most egalitarian of faiths.

(39) Is Islam as violent as it is perceived to be in the West?

Contrary to the opinion commonly held in the West, Islam, though for centuries the religion of conquering peoples, was historically spread by the word, not by the sword. This is what made it possible for Judaism to flourish in the Muslim world for centuries, and for Christianity to continue flourishing in a number of Arab countries to the present day. This is also what made it possible for Christianity, for example, to remain the religion of Spain, and for Hinduism to remain the dominant religion in the Indian subcontinent, despite centuries of Muslim rule. The European Christian dictum *cuius regio eius religio* (Whose religion, his [the ruler's] religion) has no Muslim equivalent.

In the Christian West, much has been made of the Muslim concept of *jihad*, commonly taken to mean 'holy war'. In the Qur'an, the verb *jahada* (exerted efforts) is used to enjoin military and financial support for the Prophet Muhammad in his conflict with the unbelieving Meccans, who opposed his mission, persecuting him and his followers.

Essentially, *jihad* involves the legitimate right of a community to defend itself by force in case of need. For example, the term in Islam was applied historically to the Muslim wars against the Crusader invaders. *Jihad*, however, does not describe wars of conquest or aggression. Even in his *jihad* against the Meccan unbelievers, the Prophet Muhammad was enjoined by the Qur'an to make peace with his enemies should they show any inclination to peace (8:61).

As already indicated, the fact that some Muslim individuals and factions in recent decades have engaged in terrorist activity, much as non-Muslims have done, does not justify the common Western association of Islam with terrorism and violence.

40 Do all Muslims practice Islam in the same manner?

The vast majority of the world's Muslims practice Islam in its mainstream form, which is called Sunni (from *Sunna* [tradition]), there being four recognized Sunni schools of law, with variations in certain matters of detail: the Hanafite, the Shafi'ite, the Malikite, and the Hanbalite (the last being the most strict and puritanical). (Those known to some people as the Wahhabis in Saudi Arabia are Sunni Muslims following the Hanbalite rite, as revived in the mid-eighteenth century by Muhammad Ibn 'Abd al-Wahhab.) Non-Sunni Muslims are known as *Shi'a* (Shi'ites), who comprise some ten percent of the world's Muslim population.

The issue that originally separated the Shi'ites from the Sunni Muslims was the question of the succession of the Prophet Muhammad in the political leadership of the *Ummah* (community of Islam). The Shi'ites maintain that the Prophet Muhammad had designated his first cousin and son-in-law Ali to be his *khalifah*, or caliph (successor); also, that the *Imamate* (legitimate leadership) of Islam remained the preserve of Ali's descendants after him, regardless of who actually held the caliphate. (Historically, Ali was the fourth caliph to succeed the Prophet Muhammad in the political leadership of Islam; but the caliphate did not pass after him to his descendants.)

The sects of Shi'ite Islam differ from one another as to what line of Alid Imams they recognize. The Zaydi Shi'ites, who survive to this day in Yemen, were originally the followers of Zayd, one of Ali's several great-grandsons. They maintain that any descendant of Ali can be the Imam of Islam, provided he succeeds in securing the Imamate. The *al-Ithna 'ashariyya* (Twelver Shi'ites) recognize the succession of twelve infallible imams in the line of Ali, the last of whom went into a *ghayba* (absence) from which he is expected to return as the *Mahdi* (Divinely-Guided One) to re-establish the legitimate Muslim order in the world. The Isma'ili Shi'ites recognize the seventh infallible imam in the line of Ali to have been Isma'il, the eldest son of the sixth imam (the last one recognized by the Twelvers and Isma'ilis alike). Having died while his father was still alive, Isma'il could not actually succeed him. According to the Isma'ilis, however, the Imamate remained the preserve of his descendants by right. These became the 'hidden' imams, the last of whom, emerging from hiding in AD 909, established the Fatimid caliphate in North Africa (so-called after Fatima, the daughter of the Prophet Muhammad and the wife of Ali). (The capital of the Fatimids was subsequently moved to Egypt, where the Fatimid dynasty continued to reign until AD 1171.)

While the Zaydi Shi'ites do not differ from mainstream Sunnite Islam except over the essentially political question of the Imamate, the Twelver and Isma'ili Shi'ites (the latter existing today in different sects) developed special theological and, to a more limited extent, juridicial doctrines to which Sunni Islam does not subscribe. Twelver Shi'ism today predominates in Iran, with followers in some other Muslim countries. Among the Isma'ilis, who form a much smaller community in the Muslim world, the majority today recognize the Aga Khan as their Imam.

41 Is there unity between Muslims all over the world?

In the Muslim view, Muslims constitute one *Ummah* regardless of any differences among them. Hence, while the Muslim world from an early time came to comprise different nations pursuing different interests, each independently of the other, a sense of Muslim community continues to exist among them. This does not mean that Muslims of different nationalities stand forever united against the rest of the world. It does mean, however, that Muslims of different parts of the world should remain concerned for one another's well being and, because of Islam's inherent universality, for others too.

The Implications of Islam for Civil Society and Democratization

On Diversity

⟨⟩ Among His signs are the creation of heaven and earth and the diversity of your tongues and colors. ⟨⟩ (30: 22)

On Belief

⟨⟩ There shall be no compulsion in religion. ⟨⟩ (2: 256)

On Judgment

⟨⟩ Your duty is only to warn them: you are not their keeper. As for those that turn their backs and disbelieve, Allah will inflict on them the supreme chastisement. To Us they shall return, and We will bring them to account. ⟨⟩ (88: 21–26)

On Coexistence

⟨⟩ Do not revile the idols which they invoke besides Allah, lest in their ignorance they should spitefully revile Allah. We have planned the actions of all men. To their Lord they shall return, and He will declare to them all that they have done. ⟨⟩ (6: 108)

On Discrimination

⟨⟩ Now Pharaoh made himself a tyrant in the land. He divided his

This chapter was first published in: *Two Cheers for Secularism*, edited by Sidney Brichto and Richard Harries (Pilkington Press, 1998), ch. 4, pp. 47–53. [Based on a lecture to the Charlemagne Institute, London, June 1996.] Reprinted in El Hassan bin Talal, *Continuity, Innovation and Change: Selected Essays*, Majlis El Hassan, The Royal Court, Amman, 2001; ch. 2, pp. 7–16.

people into castes, one group of which he persecuted, putting their sons to death and sparing their daughters. Truly, he was an evildoer. ◉〗 (28: 4)

The wave of democratization unleashed by the end of the Cold War has fundamentally transformed the political landscape in every part of the globe. More people than ever before are casting ballots to determine their own futures. Political participation and public accountability are the watchwords of the present era. However, underpinning this tremendous surge of political change is the phenomenon known as civil society.

In contemporary political philosophy, civil society needs democratic social interaction. It exists outside the boundaries of the family, but lies short of the state. It involves organizing virtually everything that happens between individual citizens and the state that is not violent. Almost any autonomous group or association which comes into existence by the will and efforts of its members may be considered part of civil society. But civil society also requires standards of behavior. Activity within civil society and tolerance to those with different views is perhaps its keystone.

The Muslim individual in civil society shares virtually the same ethic – the same notion of what is good and needs to be done, and what is evil and needs to be avoided – as people of other traditions. In many ways, even the idea of the modern Muslim state, irrespective of its geographic specificity or civilizational legacy, is based upon principles that most Muslims already recognize as being an inherent component of their structure of belief within a modern world: a secure sense of identity; respecting the rights of minority communities and promoting a culture of tolerance toward cultures that are different from that of the majority population; respect for rule of law; promotion of multiculturalism, and racial and ethnic integration; equality and equity in all spheres to ensure the smooth – though not uniform – functioning of society based upon individual and communal awareness of the inherent dignity of others; and everyone's right to live in a society free from fear and prejudice.

In the Qur'an there is no concept of war of aggression and no concept of permissiveness of violence. Even where permission of war has been given, it has only been given to defend and protect rights of the oppressed and exploited, not for achieving power. There is no verse in the Qur'an which permits violence for conquering territory or for achieving power. In fact, war has been qualified by the words *fī sabīlillah* (in the way of Allah).

And what is the way of Allah? Allah's way is of justice; Allah's way is of protecting the rights of the poor and exploited. Time and again the Qur'an shows its sympathy for the weaker sections of the society, in which it includes, among others, orphans, widows, slaves, the poor and the exploited, and other politically or socially disadvantaged or oppressed people. It emphasizes different ways of helping them. Allah's way is based on grounds of compassion – sensitivity to others' suffering. People cannot be compassionate unless they are responsive to the suffering of others. And this suffering includes not only that of human beings, but also that of animals and plants.

Some scholars believe that civil society is either absent or ineffective in the Muslim world. They claim that Muslim countries, and the Middle East in particular, have no part in the global process of democratization. Those who hold this view usually see Islam as an obstacle to the emergence of participatory and pluralist politics. They argue that nothing in Islamic tradition resembles the idea of representative government, or the notion of society as composed of various autonomous, self-activating groups and associations. Claiming that autocracy and acquiescence are the dominant traditions of Islamic history, such scholars generally conclude that any present or future Muslim community will almost by definition lack a vibrant civil society and participatory system of government.

However, a growing number of scholars are now questioning the idea that the Muslim world lacks the ability to achieve more inclusive political processes. They point to historical and contemporary evidence to show that both the organization and the standards of behavior of civil society are present in the Muslim world. Such scholars conclude that there are indeed good prospects for more representative governments.

For my part, I believe that this second perspective is much closer to reality. I believe that the Muslim world has always known activities as well as standards of behavior that are characteristic of civil society. Long before the 'discovery' of the New World, Muslim civilization was a melting pot of cultures and races. It is no romanticization to recall that the Muslim world was, before the advent of the world of nation-states, a place where those fleeing religious or intellectual persecution in their own lands could find sanctuary; a corner of the planet where religion supported scientific advances; where as much care was taken to respect the environment as was taken to maintain social order – not by compulsion (for there is no compulsion in religion, especially in matters of law and order), but by education and a sense of civic responsibility; where diversity was celebrated; and where enlightenment was underscored by a sense of ethics in all spheres of life. Thus civil society and Islam have always had an integrative, organic, and harmonious relationship.

I believe that the outlook for the future is promising. Of course, Westminster-style democracy has not, as yet, established firm roots throughout the Muslim world. But I would suggest that commentators who reject the possibility of civil society and democratization are overlooking a gradual but nevertheless ongoing process of evolution that is changing our region as comprehensively as any revolution, with perhaps more enduring effects.

To make this case, I will first discuss the Islamic tradition, especially as it relates to the standards of behavior of civil society. I will then move on to survey some contemporary trends in the Muslim world as they relate to its organization.

Muslims believe that Islam embodies the complete truth about human existence. Those who say that Islam and civil society are incompatible claim that belief systems which profess to be sole custodians of the truth are seldom disposed toward tolerance and pluralism. However, this critique overlooks the fact that an intrinsic part of the Islamic conception of truth is its acknowledgment of, and respect for, diversity. Indeed, it is this which has allowed Islam to grow and to enrich itself over the centuries by drawing on the deep wellspring of human variety.

The Muslim world is looking at itself very seriously and is moving toward democratic transition. But it needs to be given the self-confidence to exist, rather than to be viewed as a conglameration of rogue states, harborers of terrorism, or dictatorships. There is no primary priority but a set of equal priorities and challenges. To suggest that democracy is somehow an easy corrective to complex problems is to fantastically oversimplify the realities and to forget at our peril our part in allowing those negative realities to fester.

Islam holds that God wills differences among human beings. The Qur'an tells us: ⟨⟨❂ Had your Lord pleased, He would have united all mankind ❂⟩⟩ (11:118). Human variety is considered to be one of the proofs of God. Muslim tradition holds that diversity – for example in our appearances, languages and so forth – is among His signs. So while Islam conceives of itself as the completion of previous religious traditions, it does not demand sterile uniformity. Rather, it commands that human beings respect and learn from each other's differences. The Qur'an says: ⟨⟨❂ O mankind! We have created you from a male and a female and divided you into nations and tribes that you might know one another ❂⟩⟩ (49:13). The Prophet Muhammad is remembered in a story describing his protection of the images of Jesus and Mary in the sacred place of the

Ka'ba. This may be read not only as an acknowledgment of religious pluralism, but also as a validation of the respect that should be accorded to mother and child in Muslim life.[9]

As with other variations, human differences in matters of belief are therefore respected by Islam. It is not for Muslims to force their beliefs on others. Islam does not condone compulsion in religion. The Qur'an is extremely emphatic in making this point: ❁ Had your Lord pleased, all the people of the earth would have believed in Him. Would you then force faith upon men? ❁ (10:99). The essential corollary of this position is the far-reaching idea that it is not humanity's place to judge the merits of different beliefs. Muslims are encouraged to engage in discussion and dialogue with non-Muslims; but judgment is the prerogative of God alone.

On the basis of these principles, Islamic tradition enjoins mutual tolerance and coexistence among and between human communities. It also stresses the equality and dignity of each and every human soul. The Prophet Muhammad is reliably reputed to have said: "All people are equal. They are as equal as the teeth on a comb. There is no claim of merit of an Arab over a non-Arab, or of a white over a black person, or a male over a female. Only God-fearing people merit a preference with God." Furthermore, the idea that rights of citizenship accrue on the basis of residence was well known to Islam. For example, the Qur'an rebukes Egypt's Pharaoh for discriminating against the Jewish community in Egypt.

Thus, Islamic teaching favors equality; respects individual and communal rights of belief and citizenship; and advocates the peaceful management of diversity. Although there are, of course, examples of behavior to the contrary, they are the exceptions; for the historical record shows that Muslim societies have in the main practiced these principles.

---

9 A. J. Wensinck [J. Jomier], KA'BA, in H. A. R. Gibb *et al.* (ed.), *The Encyclopedia of Islam* (new edition: Leiden, 1960–), IV, p. 320.

The earliest practical illustration of these principles is a document known as the Constitution (or Charter) of Medina, which articulated the agreements concluded between the Prophet Muhammad and the non-Muslim tribes of Medina. The Constitution enabled each party to keep its own laws and customs. It conferred rights and obligations of citizenship among members of the community on the basis of residence and religious belief. The Constitution of Medina is thus at base a civil code and a blueprint for Islamic pluralism. Indeed, according to Dr. Azizah al-Hibri, an Islamic legal scholar,

> "it is readily apparent that there are significant parallels between the concepts expressed in the Charter of Medina, executed in the seventh century, and those of the American Constitution, drafted in the eighteenth century in that the Medina Constitution provided freedom of religion and constitutional rights and responsibilities for the Muslims and the non-Muslim counterparts on an equal footing."[10]

According to this Constitution, the Prophet Muhammad himself did not issue commands relating to the city, but consulted with the clan leaders before coming to an agreement with them. His continuing success as a leader and a settler of disputes, and other leaders' increasing respect for his judgment, were what gave the Prophet authority – not military force or invoking any idea of inherent rights of governance.[11]

In later times, the *millet* system of the Ottoman Empire granted non-Muslims a concrete bill of rights and empowered them to run their own communal affairs. Under this system, non-Muslim communities paid a poll tax in return for exemption from the obligation of *jihad*. They

---

10 "Islamic and American Constitutional Law: Borrowing Possibilities or a History of Borrowing?" *Journal of Constitutional Law,* University of Pennsylvania, vol. 1:3, Spring 1999.
11 Gibb, *The Encyclopedia of Islam,* V, 996.

were eligible for all but the very highest executive positions. In every other respect they had the same worldly rights and obligations as Muslims. These norms can be seen as a solid basis for civil society in the Muslim world. However, there are also many organizational precedents in Muslim history which should be considered.

Traditional Muslim society was ordered around a central political authority, combining temporal and spiritual affairs; but public space was immediately shared by a variety of collective associations. These included the merchants, guilds, *ulama'*, Muslim and non-Muslim sects and tribes. Some of these groupings enjoyed considerable autonomy from central government in terms of power as well as resources. They ran most of their own internal affairs through elected or appointed leaders, elders and notables, known as *Ahlu al-Ḥal wa al-'akd* (the Solvers and Binders). It was their responsibility to manage intra-communal affairs and inter-communal conflicts. They represented the interests of the people in general and their own constituencies in particular to the central authority, while conveying and legitimizing the central authority's decisions to their constituencies. Central authority collected taxes, administered justice, and maintained public order and defense. However, it was not expected to provide social services or to exercise direct economic functions. These were mostly left to local communities, which were grouped according to primordial, religious, ethnic and occupational solidarities. Thus, traditional Muslim societies relied on communal formations for many of their political and economic needs as well as for identity.

It should also be recalled that trade was central to Muslim society and that various civil society mechanisms evolved to facilitate it. The Middle East has the longest recorded history of civil and private law regarding the rights and property of the trader. The contractual forms in which such rights are expressed were probably also pioneered in the region. Although interest-based groups such as trade associations may have originated elsewhere, they rose to prominence in the medieval Muslim world. The ancient role of the guilds is especially noteworthy in having provided not only business links, but also various opportunities to undertake charitable donorship, patronage, and social security programs.[12] Just like their successor organizations of the present day, such as chambers of commerce, they enjoyed considerable success in lobbying central authority on behalf of their members' interests, whether or not those interests coincided with the policy goals of the government.

But perhaps what made such processes unique in the Islamic context was their ethical dimension. Historically, global integration in Islam is not a runaway assimilative process but a responsible movement toward recognizing what unites humanity in terms of our concerns as human beings; it then allows humanity to devise ways toward a reassessment of our priorities, working toward the greater common good and constructing new paradigms of positive action and responsibility in our relations (be they economic, social, political, cultural, and so on).

This brings me to the present-day Muslim world and the question of whether credible and accessible mechanisms exist for citizens and communities to organize themselves according to their interests and to convey their views to government.

As one might expect from the religious and historical background outlined above, a wide variety of interest-based groups do exist in today's Muslim world. Although they seldom receive attention in the West, countless political parties, religious groups, press and professional associations, and trade unions function outside the government in virtually every Muslim country. Innumerable voluntary organizations, human rights bodies, women's associations, minority rights groups and social organiza-

---

12 It is regrettable that individual 'Zakat Funds' have in many cases been closed down. Perhaps now is the time to propose the establishment of an International Zakat Foundation toward the implementation of charitable works, educational schemes, and sustainable development projects.

tions are to be found throughout the region. Citizens are constantly meeting, both formally and informally, to discuss issues that concern them – ranging from local health and education to national economic and foreign policy – and to organize ways in which to put their views to the government. We find inspirational examples of active civil society in very recent establishments such as the Grameen Bank, which originated in Bangladesh, and the Katchi Abadis housing projects in Pakistan.[13] Some governments welcome such activity; others do not. In both cases, however, activities of this nature continue and they cannot be stopped.

At the grassroots of Muslim culture, civil society organizations are thriving. Democratization and transparent, accountable governmental practices are beginning to take hold. I believe that the prospects for the future are indeed promising. I say this on the basis of studies that are coming out of Jordan, Turkey, North Africa, the Arabian Gulf, Indonesia, Malaysia, and so forth. The immense range of civil society organizations that emerges from such studies proves that Muslim citizens are willing and able to play a direct role in shaping the policies that govern their lives. Islam is not an obstacle to reform. On the contrary, Islamic teaching and tradition provide solid bases for the development of civil society. Civility and citizenship, tolerance and pluralism are fundamental to Islamic tradition. These perspectives are increasingly being articulated by Muslim thinkers who are drawing on the best of this tradition to develop positive and progressive interpretations of Islam.

Unfortunately, these vital developments appear to have little impact on the global image of contemporary Islam. Ian Buruma, writing in *The Guardian* (May 21, 2002), states that "Muslims have a harder time entering the mainstream of European societies" compared to people of other religious non-Christian denominations. Perceptions of the Muslim world

---

13 More information may be found through links at http://www.grameen-info.org/ (Grameen Bank) and http://www.skaa.cutecity.com/ (Katchi Abadis).

are extremely distorted. The general contempt that the Western media often display toward Islam exacerbates the situation. While images of Muslim religious extremism are burned into the Western consciousness, they are by no means universally accepted in the Muslim world as models of piety. Yet alternative models of Islamic leadership, which pursue a path of tolerance, pluralism, and moderation, are not widely known in the West.

Yasmin Alibhai-Brown argues that "To ignore reformist Muslims is to abandon hope for any of us in the future."[14] She defines reformists as "people who see that there are universal principles of rights, freedoms, democracy and justice which apply as much to Muslims as others ... people insulted by the idea that they must be 'tolerated' and who have the brains and guts to engage fully as democratic citizens." Indeed, she emphatically suggests that none of Islam's fundamental principles is incompatible with belief in free choice, gender equality, democracy, and a secular state.

It should be acknowledged that some figures from the Muslim world have tried to initiate a global dialogue at various levels. For my part, I have been involved in inter-cultural and inter-faith initiatives for many years, and have always sought to put forward the progressive Muslim perspective. However, it is regrettable that such initiatives never receive the kind of media coverage that violent acts receive. One cannot help but feel a sense of frustration; for much depends on the success of such initiatives, and their success depends largely on their public recognition.

---

14 "Reformist Muslims are bringing new hope to Islam," *The Independent*, September 9, 2002.

Postscript
Toward a Universal Ethic of Human Understanding

As one of those consulted on the recent United Nations Dialogue of Civilizations process, and as a Muslim, my belief is that in constructing a new paradigm of global relations, we need also to construct a complementary discipline of anthropolitics, a politics of humanity. The Declaration of the World's Parliament of Religion, *A Global Ethic*, for example, strives to establish a moral ground for human actions. The four basic principles of a Global Ethic are close to the notion of natural rights –and form a minimum common ethical understanding. Today, more than at any other time in the past, an ethic of human solidarity and a new international humanitarian order is needed. Both these processes – dialogue among civilizations and a global ethic – have, if not their origins in modern Islamic thinking, at least an integrated and inherent Islamic component.

Today, it is imperative to resolve disputes peacefully. The alternative entails an unwelcome arms race with a parallel reduction in economic and social development, and a slowing down of the progress toward soft security; that is, human dignity and human needs. A visible outcome of this is the migration of people out of a conflict-ridden region to other regions where they can have a chance to realize their aspirations in security and a decent human environment. Human migration, however, is a loss for any region, especially one undergoing changes and transitions at various levels.

A new thinking is needed: one based upon the interconnections and interdependence between peoples, while respecting diversity. Such new thinking in relation to what might traditionally be described as developing countries or the Third World (or perhaps more appropriately the "emerging world"), ought also to consider the interrelation between energy, arms and debt, and how this nexus of insanity prevents a guaranteed peaceful and sustainable future.

Some of the basic concepts need to be revisited. For instance, might we not redefine poverty in terms of human well-being rather than in terms of monetary wealth? The emerging world could lead the way by humanizing economics and politics, putting human well-being at the center of national, as well as global, policymaking. Do we need wars to remind ourselves of our common humanity? Why can the defenses for peace not be built in peacetime? Why have international efforts been devoted in recent decades more to peacekeeping than peacemaking? Can we not speak of crisis prevention rather than crisis management, as though the management of a crisis is an end in itself?

Until terrorism has a universally accepted definition, a 'war against terror' will equally be ill-defined. Terrorism thrives on the very use of brute force supposed to stamp it out. But this is an argument that has apparently fallen on unresponsive ears. Religious leaders and civil society have not yet moved effectively in lobbying for a culture of compliance with international human rights and humanitarian law.

Pursuit of a core agreement, a universal set of common values, is now not only desirable but also urgent. Without international consensus and international compliance with humanitarian norms, there can be no unified stance against the international threat that is terrorism today – nor, indeed, a unified stance on any other global issue such as poverty, migration, environmental degradation, or conflict. The particulars of political expediency do not translate from one government to the next; a

44

commonality must be found outside military and economic solutions dominated by political variables.

My reaction to the violent acts of September 11, 2001, Bali, Moscow, Saudi Arabia, and all the other acts since then that we may describe as international terrorism, has been one of sympathy (for the victims), outrage (at the audacity of the perpetrators to hijack my religion), sadness (at the futility of it all), anger (the urge to react), and contemplation (the blessing of being able to rationalize that baser desire to react). As a Muslim, I believe God does not order men to commit evil deeds.

Humanity therefore has to lay the groundwork for the adoption of a new mindset in which combating poverty, racism, terrorism, inequality, hatred, and intolerance becomes a moral imperative in us all. We have to give future generations – especially the young – some constructive hope as well as the inspiration that it is possible to build not merely a new world order but a new world attitude. The moral imperative is the ethic of human understanding that I continue to stress. It is a policy framework for human interaction and inter-existence – a universal ethic of human understanding.

The immense challenge facing us all is whether we can manage the transition from a culture of war to a culture of peace. The Qur'an repeatedly calls on us to observe "the perpetual change of winds" (2:164), "the alternation of day and night" (2:164), "the variety of human colors and tongues" (30:22), and "the alternation of days of success and reverse among peoples" (30:140) – to contemplate our place in the totality of creation and to accept that it is beautiful for its diversity. We have to understand the cultures of others and respect them. This includes a fundamental grasp of what I like to refer to as the 'anthropology of suffering'. We must become sensitized to the fact that we all carry psychological and historical baggage that has to be addressed and acknowledged if we are to make true peace with one another.

Jalal ud-Din er-Rumi, one of the greatest poets of the Islamic world, born in Afghanistan in the thirteenth century, wrote:

Come now whoever you are!
Come without any fear of being disliked.
Come whether you are a Muslim, a Christian or a Jew.
Come whoever you are!
Whether you believe or do not believe in God.
Come also if you believe in the sun as God.
This door is not a door of fear.
This is a door of good wishes.

Islamic Societies and Prospects for Democratization

DAVID L. BOREN

Islam is a fast growing religion in the United States, both because of immigration and conversions, and Muslim Americans contribute greatly and positively to all aspects of our national life. However, the interest of most Americans in Islam today is not as a faith to which they might like to convert but centers chiefly on whether, as one of the world's higher religions,[15] Islam has within its broad body of sacred writings and theology the beliefs, principles, and tolerance toward those of other faiths and secular groups: (1) to live in peace, harmony, and cooperation with non-Islamic countries; and (2) to allow for the creation of democratic, just societies with accountable governments within Islamic states. In short, the question for many Americans and peoples of the English language is whether the practice and dynamics of Islam are compatible with world peace and democracy.

These concerns are grounded in the broad desire for peace and also freedom from unjust violence. They are also grounded in the intrinsic belief of Americans in democracy and in the inalienable rights of all humankind. The two are interconnected because Americans believe that democratic states are less belligerent with other democratic states, and that

I wish to express my appreciation to Ambassador Edwin G. Corr of the University of Oklahoma, Professor Dale F. Eickelman of Dartmouth University, and Professor Wadad Kadi of the University of Chicago, for material and ideas they provided for my writing of this chapter.

15 I am using the term "higher religion" here in the sense employed by Arnold Toynbee in *An Historian's Approach to Religion* (Oxford University Press, 1956).

they allow their citizens and other persons residing within their borders greater opportunity to pursue life, liberty, and happiness.

His Royal Highness Prince El Hassan bin Talal's exposition on the essence of Islam as a faith argues that within Islam are essential truths and principles upon which Muslims can build democratic societies. He also argues that there is a growing civic society within many Islamic states that augurs well for Muslims to advance to fully democratic states.

The Freedom House Report of 2002 stated that the number of freely elected governments had climbed to 121 out of 192 independent countries,[16] and a July 2002 United Nations Development Program (UNDP) *Human Development Report* also reported the continued expansion of the number of democratic countries.[17] Thus far, Islamic states have not figured significantly in compilations of nations in the world's growing democratization. Nevertheless, Prince El Hassan's logic, his examples of specific expressions of the Qur'an, and the history of earlier Islamic empires, provide a basis for optimism that mainstream Islam can be respectful of non-Muslims and diversity.

To have a balanced view it is necessary to examine not only the extremists and violent movements within Islam during the last quarter century but also take into account the central teachings of Islam and the total history and scope of a religion fourteen centuries old. An objective examination reveals long periods of moderation and tolerance (for instance in Spain and Sicily). The view of some westerners that Muslims are inherently intolerant comes from a concept of how Muslims regard their practice of *jihad* – as being only the military conquest of infidels (non-Muslims). In contrast to this image of Islam as having been

---

16 Adrian Karatnycky, general editor, Aili Piano, managing editor, *Freedom in the World: The Annual Survey of Political Rights and Civil Liberties, 2001–2002* (New Jersey: Transaction Publishers, Rutgers, 2002), p. 7.

17 *Human Development Report, 2002* (New York: United Nations Publications, 2002).

characterized by intolerance, Mark Cohen notes "That Jews of Islam, especially during the formative and classical centuries (up to the thirteenth century) experienced far less persecution than did the Jews of Christiandom."[18]

His Royal Highness points out that the Constitution of Medina, written and promulgated by the Prophet Muhammad for the multi-religious ten thousand-strong city state in AD 622 was for a plural society and gave citizens equal rights and a say in government matters:

> "The Constitution of Medina, which articulated the agreements concluded between Sayyidina Muhammad and the non-Muslim tribes of Medina … not only enabled each party to keep its own laws and customs, but conferred rights and obligations of citizenship among members of the community on the basis of residence and religious belief. The Constitution of Medina is thus at base a civil code and blueprint for Islamic pluralism. In later times the millet system [of the Ottoman Empire] granted non-Muslims a bill of rights and empowered them to run their own internal affairs."[19]

The Egyptian democracy activist Saad Eddin Ibrahim, who in 2003 won the 'Muslim Democrat of the Year' award, insists that true Islam is fully compatible with democracy. He, along with other Muslim advocates of democracy, joins Prince El Hassan in his focus on the Charter of Medina as a fundamental Islamic document and experience upon which Muslims

---

18 Daniel Pipes, "The Evil Isn't Islam," *The New York Post*, July 20, 2002. Pipes is drawing upon Mark Cohen's book *Judaism Under the Cresent and the Cross* (Princeton: Princeton University Press, 1994). See also Carol Griffith (ed.), *Islam: A Primer, A Conversation with Roy Mottahedeh and Jay Tolson*, in Center Conversations, No. 15, September 2002, published by The Ethics and Public Policy Center, Washington, D.C.

19 Prince El Hassan bin Talal, "A New World Order without Ideologies," in a speech delivered as President of the Club of Rome to the Swiss Federal Institute, Zurich, Switzerland, February 4, 2003. See also the Prince's comments on the Constitution of Medina (p. 38).

can justify and build democratic political systems. Ibrahim says the Charter contains "all the aspects of pluralism, which is the prerequisite for democracy." Through the Charter, the Prophet Muhammad laid down the principle of "equality in worldly matters" with fourteen non-Muslim groups living in Medina some five hundred years before the Magna Carta was written.[20]

There are, as Prince El Hassan points out in this book, many teachings within Islam that can be drawn upon in creating more democratic societies. Ali Mazrui, the Chair of the Center for the Study of Islam and Democracy (CSID) that bestowed the award upon Ibrahim, argues that "some democratic principles have been part of Islam from the beginning." The CSID president, Radwan Masmoudi, cautioned that it is necessary to convince political and religious leaders and the masses in the Islamic world that democracy is compatible with Islam; because if Muslims feel they have to choose between democracy and Islam, the majority will choose Islam, but it would be a false choice.[21]

Respected observers of the worldwide democratization process support the view that Islam contains the values upon which democracies can be constructed, although there are some naysayers and doubters. Samuel Huntington, in *The Third Wave: Democratization in the Late Twentieth Century* called to our attention the seemingly inevitable expansion of democracy among the nations since 1828, notwithstanding important reversals. Huntington points out that egalitarianism and volunteerism are central themes of Islam. He cites Ernest Gellner who has argued that Islam's features of "unitarianism, a rule-ethic, individualism, spiritualism, Puritanism, an egalitarian aversion to meditation and hierar-

---

20 Ralph Dannheisser, "Saad Eddin Ibrahim Urges Democracy for the Muslim World," "Washington File," May 19, 2003, a product of the Bureau of International Information Programs, US Department of State. Web site: http://usinfo.state.gov.

21 *Ibid.*

chy are congruent with modernization." Huntington says these character-istics are also congruent with democracy, although he expresses concern about Islam's rejection of a distinction between religious and apolitical communities, and the insistence of many Muslims that *Shari'a* (literally, the "way" or "path" for human conduct to understand God; law from the Qur'an and *Ḥadīth*) should be the basic law of countries and the *ulama'* (literally, the learned people; Muslim clergy) should at least review and ratify all government policy.[22]

The intent of some Muslims, perhaps the majority, is to try to turn *Shari'a* into a singularly comprehensive political framework, constitution, and platform for their countries in this modern age. The fact that many Muslim peoples want the *Shari'a* to be the basic law of their countries and for the *ulama'* have the ultimate word over government policy and prac-tice is a difficult one for Americans and for Western democratic theoreti-cians. The idea of religion and government being one is a concept that leaves most Americans with a picture of theocratic authoritarianism with little to no room for secularism and individual freedom in thought and action, or it leaves an image of secular authoritarian rulers using religion and religious institutions to maintain power and achieve secular ends. Generally, Americans accept that religion has a vital role in American life and politics, but that, properly, faith and beliefs are instilled in individu-als by their families, friends, and various religious institutions. Individuals carry these values with them in their judgments and actions in the politi-cal arena as individuals. Religious institutions themselves, though indi-rectly very important in America's political life, are restricted in exercising directly political power and execution of political policies and programs.

---

22 Samuel P. Huntington, *The Third Wave: Democratization in the Late Twentieth Century* (Norman and London: University of Oklahoma Press, 1991), p. 307; see also Ernest Gellner, "Up from Imperialism," *The New Republic*, May 22, 1989, pp. 35–36. For a better understanding of *Shari'a,* see John Alden Williams (ed.), *Islam* (New York: George Braziller, 1962), pp. 92–135.

Both religion and politics, Americans hold, have their distinct realms, even though they sometimes overlap and the boundaries between them are not always clearly defined. The concept of some degree of separation of church and state as being essential to a functioning democracy has long been a revered principle in the United States, even though the separation currently seems to be narrowing.

Americans also question the application today of some parts of the *Shari'a*, just as they would the application of some of the laws of the Torah and the Old Testament in general. Practices such as costly and complicated arrangements to avoid the appearance of paying bank interest, the death penalty, stoning for adultery, honor killings, and clerical death sentences for execution by believers against blasphemers and apostates are neither understood nor approved by most Americans. Disturbing to Americans are the edicts of some Islamic countries which ban Christian crosses, churches, Bibles, and the open practice of religions other than Islam. These prohibitions seem contrary to the values of hospitality and tolerance taught in the Qur'an and those that have characterized most of Islamic history and governance such as those practiced in medieval Spain.[23]

The Prince emphasizes in his responses to questions 21 and 23 in the 'To Be A Muslim' chapter that in Islam decisions regarding such practices as dress by women, diet, and life styles vary greatly and are the responsibility of the individual believer. He points out that there is tremendous diversity of practice among Muslim communities and individual Muslims. Many Americans seldom focus on those Islamic countries – such as Jordan, Mali, and Qatar – where there is substantial tolerance, diversity, and freedom.

---

23 Maria Rosa Menocal, *The Ornament of the World: How Muslims, Jews, and Christians Created a Culture of Tolerance in Medieval Spain* (New York, NY: Little, Brown and Company, 2003).

It is important to point out with respect to the *ulama'*, except for the Shi'ites who constitute about ten percent of all Islam, that Muslim clergy do not have the same kind of hierarchy and unity that is common in many Christian denominations. This lack of organizational structure decreases the coherence and power of the *ulama'* within a society. Separation of church and state in the West, in large part, grew out of the Protestant Reformation. There are distinguished and respected students of Islam, such as Dale Eickelman, who claim that a 'reformation' is taking place in the Islamic world, which is having a tremendous impact on Muslims and how they look at their own clergy, governments, and the non-Muslim world. Eickelman cautions that this 'Muslim reformation' is very different from the sixteenth-century Christian protestant reformation but could have a similar major impact. It derives in part from the increasing level of education, the opening up for Muslims of new sources of information about the world, and the breaking down of old lines of religious and secular authority.

Other scholars, such as Robin Wright and John Esposito, also assert that Islam is currently undergoing some kind of a reformation. Like His Royal Highness, the reformers believe in a strong Islamic civic society and in some form of democracy. Roy Mottahadeh says that Islamic reformers are looking for something like a state's recognition of Islam as its official religion in the same way that European governments have recognized a single Christian denomination, though allowing freedom of worship to others and not demanding the application of Islamic law to everybody.[24] Robin Wright, reviewing Gilles Kepel's *Jihad: The Trail of Political Islam*, says:

> "In the West, Christianity went through a reformation that paved the way for the Age of Enlightenment and the birth of modern democracy – a 400-year course that is still not quite

---

24 Carol Griffith (ed.), *Islam: A Primer*, pp. 2–5, and 8.

complete. Islam is now just beginning to struggle with its own reformation, a process of reinterpreting the Koran and blending religious traditions with modern society. The past quarter century of militancy is a part of this broader process – a phase of history that is definitely not over."[25]

The Prince's essay on 'The Implications of Islam for Civil Society and Democratization' shows that civic organizations and private institutions are far more developed in many countries of the Islamic world than most Westerners appreciate. The essential question regarding civic society is the degree of independence and autonomy non-governmental organizations and private institutions have from government control and to what extent the legal guarantees of freedom and non-interference in civic society are observed.

The *Arab Human Development Report, 2002*, the first such report on this region issued by the UNDP, includes encouraging findings of substantial progress in human development among the twenty-two Arab countries of the Islamic world that enhance the development of civic society. During the past three decades, life expectancy increased by about fifteen years, mortality rates for children under five years fell by about two-thirds, adult literacy almost doubled, women's literacy trebled, there have been large increases in education enrollments (including of girls), daily calorie intake and access to safe water are higher, and "the incidence of poverty is lower than of any other developing region."[26] The pioneer-

---

25 Robin Wright, "Mosque and State: A French academic argues that the militant Islamic theocracy movement has run its course," *The New York Times Book Review*, Sunday, May 26, 2002, p. 8, in which Wright reviews Gilles Kepel, *Jihad: The Trail of Political Islam* (Cambridge, MA: Harvard University Press, 2002)

26 Mark Mallock Brown, "Foreword by the Administrator, UNDP" in *Arab Human Development Report 2002: Creating Opportunities for Future Generations*, published by The United Nations Development Program (UNDP), sponsored by the Regional Bureau for ARAB States of the UNDP and the Arab Fund for Economic and Social Development (New York: United Nations Publications, 2002), p. iv.

ing two dozen Arab scholars who wrote the *Report* lamented, however, that "the wave of democracy that transformed governance in most of the world has barely reached the Arab states; and that this freedom deficit undermines human development and is one of the most painful manifestations of lagging political development."[27] The Report and the Arab scholars who prepared it reflect the commitment of a new, moderate generation of intellectuals from the Islamic world to move their countries to modernization and democracy.

Hope for the Islamic world's progress in democratization and development, despite the fact that Islamic states have lagged behind other regions during almost two centuries, can be gained by looking at some of the historical studies of the relationship between democracy and Roman Catholicism. Samuel Huntington in *The Third Wave* argues that while Roman Catholicism was an impediment to democratization during this first wave (1828–1926) and the second wave (1943–63), by the third wave (1974–present) the Roman Catholic Church not only had ceased to be an obstacle but also had become a strong facilitating force for the establishment of democracy.[28] It is possible to extrapolate from this that the higher religions of the world have within their broad, deep sacred writings and theologies the values and principles upon which democracy can flourish, if adherents are committed to emphasizing those values and making them the prevailing current of their faiths.

Judgments about the slow progress of democratization in Islamic countries must also take into account their late emergence as nation-states. Nearly the entire Islamic world was in an imperial or colonial status during much of the period since 1828 when Huntington says the modern democratization process began. Moreover, it is important to

---

27 *Arab Human Development Report 2002*, p. 2.
28 Huntington, *The Third Wave*, pp. 75–85.

note that the view of Islam as being an impediment to democratization and world peace was not deeply and widely held in the West until the jolting Iranian revolution of the octogenarian Shia' religious leader Ayatollah Ruhollah Khomeini. His Shi'ite and political movement chased Shah Mohammed Reza Pavlevi into exile and established a radical theocratic government that took 69 hostages from the American Embassy and held most of them for 444 days. The shock of the United States over this experience helped to shape the current impression of Islam in much of the West. Subsequent violent events executed by Islamic extremists, some of which are mentioned in Ambassador Perkins' 'A Clash of Civilizations?', have reinforced this impression. The Iranian religious revolution was part of a minority, radical movement within the totality of Islam that had begun in the 1930s, emerged strongly in the 1970s, thrived during the 1980s and early 1990s, and may have began to subside in most countries by the late 1990s.[29]

During the 1960s and much of the 1970s there was considerable discussion among American academics, especially by those in the field of political development, about democratization throughout the developing world, including in Islamic countries. US aid programs were aimed at implanting and promoting democracy in many countries, including those with majority Islamic populations; for example, in Pakistan there was much talk about building a democratic country on the basis of "village democracy." Prince El Hassan notes that:

> "The vision of Muhammad Ali Jinah [the father of modern Pakistan] of a modern Islamic state is that of a welfare state that draws its inspiration from the principles and teachings of Islam and is founded on democratic foundations that guard and respect the individual, and offer men, women, and children

29 See Robin Wright, "Mosque and State."

equal rights regardless of their religious beliefs and political views. It is a model that we should emulate."[30]

A strong element in the thought and programs for democratization both by Islamic nationalists and American leaders was that of the secularization of the state and the separation of governmental and religious functions. Based on the Turkish experiment begun by the Mustapha Kemal Ataturk revolution in the 1920s, developmentalists in the 1960s and early 1970s regarded the secularization of Iran and Egypt and of the Ba'athist states of Syria and Iraq as positive movements toward the establishment of more liberal states.

The perception of progress toward more liberal societies changed with the already mentioned 1979 Iranian revolution and the rise of strong Islamic-based political parties and movements throughout much of the Islamic world. Their growing strength was apparent both in some governments and in opposition parties and movements from the repressive Taliban government in Afghanistan during the 1990s to the menacing opposition Islamic political parties in Algeria where in 1992 the Armed Forces aborted elections to keep the Islamic fundamentalists from taking power "democratically," along with a civil war that cost 100,000 lives. The dilemma was that honest democratic elections rather than leading to liberal, pro-western democracy seemed to have become a path by which undemocratic, radical Islamic fundamentalist movements could take power and afterward establish undemocratic theocracies.

Notwithstanding this, the democracy award winner and sociologist Sa'ad Eddin Ibrahim argues for persistence:

---

30 Prince El Hassan bin Talal, "The View of a Modern Arab Intellectual," published in the London-based daily *Al-Hayat*, excerpts of which were published by The Middle East Media Research Institute (MEMRI), Washington, D.C., and distributed on September 10, 2002 by email memri@memri.org. See also *Al Muntada* [A Quarterly Published by the Arab Thought Forum, Amman], vol. 9, no. 11, September 2002, p. 8.

"Democracy has spread through almost every region of the world, and it can take hold in the Middle East as well. Surveys show that average Arabs hunger for greater freedom and reform of the failed regimes that rule them. Islamic movements are a minority and won't win elections; if they do, they can be obliged to follow democratic rules. ..."

"There are obstacles but they can be overcome if you believe in change, in the possibility of change, and the necessity of change, and you work for it. ... You persist, and ... you ultimately triumph. It happened in the Soviet Union. It happened in Eastern Europe. It can happen anywhere."[31]

As Ambassador Perkins discusses in his 'A Clash of Civilizations?', despite the activism of militant extremist Islam so evident since the 1979 Iranian revolution, the September 11, 2001 attack by Osama bin Laden-inspired terrorists on the United States, three years of *Intifada* in Palestine and Israel, the US military action in Afghanistan against the Taliban and Osama bin Laden, and the US-led coalition war against Saddam Hussein, there are experts who believe the violent extremist elements of Islam have been in decline since the late 1990s. This, coupled with the growing strength of civic society and an increasing number of elections and legislative bodies and councils in the Islamic world, may bode well for progress in democratization and peace negotiations in the Islamic world. While searching for a basis for optimism, we must, however, admit that the path before us is far from clear. Much will depend upon determined leadership by Muslim and non-Muslims alike.

There was an opening after the 1991 Gulf War that made possible the Madrid Meeting (1991), the Oslo Accords (1993), and the achievement of

---

31 Jackson Diehl, "A Bet on Truth From Egypt," *The Washington Post National Weekly Edition*, May 26–June 1, 2003, p. 26.

the Jordanian–Israeli Peace Agreement (1994). Negotiations between the Israelis and Palestinians at Camp David and Taba almost resulted in a peace agreement. If developments in Iraq after the war there in 2003 do not further embitter the Islamic world toward the United States, and should substantial progress be achieved on the Quartet's (the United States, the European Union, Russia, and the United Nations) 'roadmap' to achieve a secure Israel and a viable Palestinian state by 2006, the environment for democratization might be even more propitious. In the near future, progress and peace in the region and a declining terrorist threat around the world are closely linked to the outcome of Israeli–Palestinian negotiations.

The Freedom House report for 2001–2002 emphasized the 'democracy gap' between countries of the Islamic world and other countries. Only 11 of 47 Islamic nations had democratically elected governments when the report was written. This meant that only 23 percent could be classified as democracies while in the non-Islamic world the percentage was over 75 percent. The report found there was considerable democratic ferment in the Islamic world, with democratic polities at that time existing in Albania, Bangladesh, Djibouti, Gambia, Indonesia, Mali, Niger, Nigeria, Senegal, Sierra Leone, and Turkey. Freedom House reported no electoral democracies among the 16 Arabic states of the Middle East and North Africa (in spite of the fact that Jordan prides itself that it is indeed an electoral democracy).

In the Middle East, democratic gains could be made in the establishment of a new Palestinian state. The Bush administration is committed to laying the groundwork for democratization in Iraq. Jordan, one of the most liberal societies in the Middle East, could make further progress toward consolidating a fully democratic constitutional monarchy, especially if there were the assurance of peace in the region and all energy could be focused on internal development. Should the situation change in

Lebanon and the people there regain full independence, there is a fairly mature civic society upon which a functioning democracy could be established. Societies have been opening in Qatar and the United Arab Emirates.[32] Iran has been progressing and now seems to have two governments – one increasingly open and democratic and the other a recalcitrant authoritarian theocracy. Turkey moved toward greater democracy with the election of an Islamic political party to the government, the Turkish military's acceptance of the new government, and that Islamic party's apparent commitment to live within the constitutional democratic framework of the country. This, of course, is key to democracy. Morocco continues with a fairly open monarchical political system, and progress toward a fully constitutional monarchy is possible.

The role and good work of the Hashemite monarchy in creating liberal societies that can move toward democracy is particularly interesting in light of the fact that one of the imminent members of that family is the author of this book. Under the British mandate, the Hashemite monarchy ruled Iraq from 1921 until 1958. If Iraq is able to democratize after the dictatorship of Saddam Hussein and the 2003 Coalition War, the country will owe much to the Hashemite family. King Faisal I of Iraq adopted a parliamentary system of government and permitted the formation of political parties. Under the Hashemites there was ample political debate and discourse in Iraq, and the development of a free press and a functioning pluralistic society. The Hashemite monarchy created a similar open and liberal society in Jordan. King Abdullah I, King Hussein, young King Abdullah II, and Prince El Hassan have all served their country well in terms of its political, social and economic development, and have been constructive and moderate voices for peace and cooperation throughout

32 Adrian Karatnycky, "The 2001–2002 Freedom House Survey of Freedom: The Democracy Gap," in Adrian Karatnycky, general editor, *Freedom in the World: The Annual Survey of Political Rights and Civil Liberties, 2001–2002*, pp. 10–17.

the region. In those Islamic countries that have monarchies, these institutions and families can be symbols of unity and tradition to hold nations together as they evolve into constitutional democracies with royal chiefs of state, or they can move their countries toward anachronistic royal absolutism.

As a final note, a viable and functioning democracy can only be achieved in a country by the leaders and people of that country. Outsiders can play an important role only if there are authentic and committed individuals and groups within the society that take leadership and responsibility for the noble endeavor. Outsiders can judiciously support such leaders but cannot dictate their actions. Only indigenous leaders and their followers can do the job. Further, as former Secretary of State Madeleine Korbel Albright reminded at the April 2003 University of Oklahoma's annual foreign policy conference, it is not in the interests of the United States or of the world to undo and upset all existing Islamic regimes and thereby create war and chaos throughout a major portion of the world.

Democratization takes time, and it makes little sense to break abruptly the historical bonds between the United States and the moderate Islamic states that have contributed to the stability of the Middle East and Islamic world for half a century. The regimes there – to varying degrees and in changing roles – played a major part in thwarting communist expansion and in containing the Islamic fundamentalist revolutionary movement after the Iranian revolution. They collaborated against Saddam Hussein during the 1991 Gulf War, and have cooperated in the war against terrorism after September 11, 2001. Democracy should be encouraged and the United States should make clear its preference for that system of government, but in the end the peoples and leaders of the Islamic world must draw upon their own values and aspirations to create for themselves free and productive societies. The Prince's superb treatise on Islam and civic society in this book demonstrates that mainline Islam is compatible with democracy and peace with the West. The conditions may be ripe for beginning a strong and sustained drive for the evolution of democratic states and societies throughout much of the Islamic world.

I call your attention to the fact that His Royal Highness is a Muslim and Jordanian. Alain Elkann is a Frenchman of the Jewish faith who has resided many years in Italy. Ed Perkins is a Roman Catholic Christian and an American. And I am an American and a Protestant Christian. This book is therefore testimony to the ability of persons of goodwill from different religious faiths and nationalities to work together in a common cause. We believe that a greater understanding by the people of the English-speaking world of what it truly means to be a Muslim and a greater understanding by Muslims of the beliefs and aspirations of Westerners will help to build a more peaceful and just world for all peoples.

In this book you have the words of one of the world's best-known leaders in the inter-faith dialogue among the religions of the globe. It is an eloquent description of what being a Muslim means to him, and to most persons who adhere to the Qur'an and the teachings of the Prophet Muhammad. We hope that this brief but important book will help you better understand one of the three major monotheistic religions and its impact on our history and on the future before us.

A Clash of Civilizations? or Normal Relations with Nations of the Islamic World?

EDWARD J. PERKINS

His Royal Highness Prince El Hassan bin Talal has argued persuasively in *To Be a Muslim: Islam, Peace, and Democracy* that the beliefs and culture of the majority of the Islamic world not only are compatible with but are contributive to a world at peace, a world of diversity, and one in which Muslim and non-Muslim nations can and should collaborate to create a more humane and just global society. He did this by citing specific verses of the Qur'an, and referring to teachings of the Qur'an, the *Ḥadīth* (sayings) and *Sunna* (tradition) of the Prophet Muhammad. He also succinctly described how most of Islam during most of its history has applied the teachings of the Prophet so as to treat other ethnic groups, cultures and faiths – especially the Jewish and Christian monotheists – with respect, tolerance, and fairness.

President Boren stated in his 'Islamic Societies' chapter that the capacity for Islamic nations to establish truly democratic systems of government is one of the major concerns of people of the West. Prince El Hassan in his explanation of what it means to be a Muslim shows that Islam is compatible with democracy, and he also describes the growth of civic society in many nations of the Islamic world as manifested by an increasing number of non-governmental organizations, autonomous institutions, and a more vigorous private sector. The values and beliefs of Islam pointed out by the Prince, and the growth of pluralism and civic society, are a base upon which more liberal and democratic societies can be created. Senator Boren reinforced the Prince's thesis that Islamic societies have the potential to join the remainder of the world's countries in their march toward democratization.

Perhaps the question about the Islamic world's capacity to achieve democracy is less critical to the West than the question of the ability of Western and Islamic nations to live together in peace and, hopefully, in harmonious cooperation. I support His Royal Highness's thesis that the Islamic religion teaches and history reveals that mainline Islam is not intrinsically aggressive toward other cultures, and that Islam's teachings are for Muslims to live in peace and cooperation with other religions, cultures, and states. The West, because of ignorance of Islam and its history, and unfortunate experiences with several Islamic nations and terrorist groups during the past quarter century, understandably has doubts about the possibility of living peacefully with the Islamic world.

These doubts and fears find expression in American academic circles in such controversial theories as Samuel Huntington's proposition that world politics and wars may become predominately a "clash of civilizations," and that the "central focus of conflict for the immediate future will be between the West and several Islamic-Confucian states."[33] Another academic example is the generally accepted thesis of Michael Doyle, who after an exhaustive study of wars since 1815, put forth as a conclusion that democratic countries are less likely to go to war against one another.[34] The root of this idea goes back at least to Immanuel Kant's eighteenth-century essay, "Perpetual Peace," in which he argued that democracies are much

---

33 Samuel P. Huntington, "The Clash of Civilizations?" *Foreign Affairs*, vol. 72, no. 3 (Summer 1993), p. 48. Huntington developed this landmark journal article into a much discussed book *The Clash of Civilizations and the Remaking of World Order*

34 Michael Doyle, "Liberalism and World Politics," *American Political Science Review*, vol. 80, no. 4 (December 1986), pp. 1151–1169.

less likely than other types of states to go to war with each other because the consent of their peoples is required.[35] The point here, in keeping with Doyle's and others' view, is a concern that because Muslim-dominated countries are less democratic as a whole than other countries, they are more likely to wage wars or become objects of aggression by democratic states.

The democracy peace thesis simply is that it is easy to find instances in history where non-democratic countries have engaged in wars with other non-democratic countries, and it is easy to encounter cases where democratic and non-democratic countries have engaged each other in wars; but it is difficult (though not impossible) to discover wars fought between democratic states. Therefore, a way to reduce if not eliminate wars would be for all states to become democratic. This, moreover, conforms to the strongly held American view that all peoples merit and have the right to live in societies with democratic and accountable govern-ments seeking the best for all sectors of their societies.

I support the Prince's argument that Islamic and Western countries can and should live with each other in peace and cooperation because:

- The Prince has convincingly presented teachings of God revealed to the Prophet Muhammad and recorded in the Qur'an that Muslims should be tolerant of and live peacefully with non-Muslims;
- History shows that since the Prophet Muhammad's death in the seventh century AD, Islamic countries and empires generally have been tolerant of minorities within their borders and at peace with other polit-ical powers; and when not at peace, it was often in response to external aggression, as during the Christian Crusades and the Mongol invasion.
- There has been a growing, virulent, aggressive, fundamentalist Islamic

---

35 Quoted in *Kant's Political Writings*, ed. Hans Reiss (Cambridge, MA: Cambridge University Press, 1970), p. 100.

political and military movement during the past quarter century that threatens secular and monarchical governments in the Islamic world and non-Muslim countries; but many experts believe the movement has run its course and is beginning to subside;

- There are promising signs that major underlying causes for resentment and aggression among this militant strain of Islam against the West may be ameliorated and diminished during the coming years by:
  - greater democratization, greater establishment of the rule of law, and increased justice in the Islamic world;
  - improvements in education, standards of living, and peoples' welfare, particularly for that half of the population that is female and will have a temporizing and 'civilizing' influence on the rest of their societies;
  - the diminution of the Israeli–Palestinian conflict through the negotiation of a peace agreement that will result in security for the State of Israel and a viable State for the Palestinians, both with defined, accepted borders.

The Prince's words about what it means to be a Muslim present the words of God to the Muslim people through His Prophet Muhammad, as recorded in the Qur'an and other sacred writings, that Muslims should abide in peace. Some of the controversy over the peaceful nature of Islam centers on the meaning of the concept of *jihad* within Islam and in the Western world. President Boren touched upon this in 'Islamic Societies'. I add here another quote from Prince El Hassan to define further the true meaning of *jihad*:

> "It is widely accepted that, like much of the developing world, Muslim societies have been stifled by their own systems of government ... the Islamic world appears to be slipping into a mindset that favors a *Jihad*ist approach in facing major chal-

lenges, but overlooks the true meaning of *Jihad*. The Greater *Jihad* in Islam is the struggle of the self. It is explicit in Islam that those who are indifferent to oppression are oppressors themselves. It is the awareness of right from wrong, good from evil, which separates the true *mujahid* from the one who loudly, though falsely, claims to be actively engaged in a *Jihad*. ...

"Our common ground [with other religions] is presently threatened by extremists on all sides who will, if given the chance, fill it with ideologies of hatred and terror in the pursuit of each other's annihilation. This type of *Jihadism* hijacks not only airplanes but religion, turning human values against humanity itself."[36]

I believe it will help the reader to comprehend the situation we now confront and the prospects for peace to have a very short description of the West's relations with the Islamic world up to World War II, followed by an account of relations with Islamic countries after most of them gained full national independence following that war. A review of relations since the emergence of significant radically fundamentalist groups in the 1970s will then help us to comprehend the situation we now confront and the chances for peace in the future. This thumbnail description of history undergirds Prince El Hassan's conviction that Islam and the West can and should live with each other peacefully and cooperatively. Before sketching the history, a few remarks about religions and some other causes for Westerners' misperceptions about Islam might be useful.

A commonly shared value among the world's higher religions is a commitment to the sanctity of life. Among most adherents of the higher religions there also has evolved, especially during the past couple

---

36 HRH Prince El Hassan bin Talal, "The Islamic World and the Trilateral Countries in the Era of Globalization," an address delivered to the Trilateral Commission Meeting, Washington, D.C., April 5–8, 2002, p. 1.

centuries, a commitment to improve the life and well-being on earth of all human beings regardless of faith, creed, or race. Nevertheless, an evaluation of any major religion or belief system begins with an acknowledgment that, while they bring meaning and value to peoples' lives by helping them to live altruistically and meaningfully and to transcend the mundane, there are, and have been, to varying degrees at different times in all religions some very evil strains. Fortunately, these strains of extremism are normally on the fringe, and when they become strong and influential, with a few notable exceptions, they eventually are restrained.

All religions have their fanatical extremist groups, and these extremists seem to mirror one another in terms of their dogmatism, need for an enemy, and the teaching of hate and destruction of that adversary. Such strains are present today in Christianity, Judaism, and Islam – not to speak of other religions as manifested by the extremist Hindus' attacks on Muslims in India. Among Christians, there are the likes of the Reverend Jerry Falwell, evangelist Pat Robertson, the Reverend Franklin Graham and the Reverend Jerry Vines, who have opened fire unreservedly on Islam and the Prophet of Islam. Among Muslims, there are not only the vitriolic attacks on the West by Osama bin Laden and promises that al-Qaeda will fight the infidels; some Friday sermons are delivered across the Muslim world by fundamentalist mullahs excoriating Western values and culture. Negative attacks on the West are also a major part of the curriculum of too many Islamic academics.[37] Among Jews, there are extremists who have attacked Muslims even when they are worshipping at their holy shrines in Jerusalem and Hebron.

While many Westerners acknowledge and appreciate Islam and an increasing number become Muslims, aside from the fundamentalists mentioned above, many moderate Americans incline to view Islam as basi-

37 Leela Jacinto, "Holy Wars? Islamic and Christian Extremists Fight a Vitriolic War of Words," ABC News Internet Ventures, January 15, 2003, <abcNews.com>.

cally hostile toward non-Muslims. This view derives in part from the history of the Prophet Muhammad's political and military struggles during his lifetime against non-Muslim foes in Mecca, and a commonly held mistaken view by many Americans that Islam was rapidly "spread by the sword" to dominate and proselytize non-Muslims throughout a large part of the world after the death of the Prophet Muhammad in AD 632. Greater knowledge about Islam and its history is required to offset these views.

The initial spread of Islam occurred over a period of more than three centuries – about the same length of time it took Christianity to become the dominant religion of the Roman Empire. Emperor Constantine's conversion in AD 312 and the "imposition" of Christianity on the Roman-ruled world could be compared to the spread of Islam through the expansion of the Islamic empires. Islam's expansion, too, was more or less gradual and conquered subjects were not individually compelled to convert. As already noted by Senator Boren in his 'Islamic Societies', the existence of Jewish and Christian minorities residing peacefully and without great harassment within the Islamic caliphates offsets the view of the rapid forceful imposition of Islam upon peoples within areas conquered militarily. After over three centuries of expansion, by AD 1000, the caliphate had diminished in authority, and in Egypt the slave-origin Mamluk dynasty ruled from 1250 to 1517.

In considering the West's view of Islam as violently aggressive and bellicose, it is also useful to recall that it was in AD 1090 that the Roman Catholic Pope Urban II, in an effort to save Eastern Christiandom from the Muslims, unleashed two hundred years of wave after wave of crusading knights that wreaked havoc, destruction, and death on the Islamic world. This occurred during Europe's 'dark ages', before the intellectual transformation of the West through the Renaissance, the Enlightenment, the Reformation, and the rise of the modern nation-state.

It was the Mamluk dynasty that finally ejected the crusaders, and then defended the Muslims against the invading Mongols. The Mongols swept out of the steppes of central Asia in the middle of the thirteenth century and killed the caliph.

By the seventeenth century Muslims had created the Ottoman Empire and were again projecting power; but in the eighteenth century it was becoming clear that European power and prosperity were surpassing that of the Muslim world. Muslims had witnessed the Crusades, the Mongol invasion, the fall of Constantinople, the ejection of the Arabs from the Iberian Peninsula, the rise of the modern nation-state and decline and end of empires, and the surge of Christian European colonialism that flowed from the Age of Exploration.

The end of empires and the end of colonialism greatly affected Eastern Europe, Africa and the Middle East, and particularly impacted on Muslim populated areas of the earth. After World War I, American President Woodrow Wilson's insistence on the "self-determination" of peoples in the establishment of nation-states as one of his Fourteen Points for the creation of a peace arrangement that would end all wars, engendered the birth of several new states. In what President Wilson described as "the whole disgusting scramble" for the Middle East,[38] the principle of self-determination was not always well applied in the drawing of borders for the new states that emerged out of the defeated Austro-Hungarian and Ottoman Empires. The creation in Islamic regions of nation-states with boundaries that encompassed disparate ethnic, tribal, and linguistic groups still causes great problems for national coherence and building a sense of nationalism. This contrasts greatly with the gradual evolution of West European and American nation-states.

The emergence in Europe of the nation-state system out of the Treaty of Westphalia in 1648 made the nation-state the major actor in

38 Ethan Broner, "Iraq and the Lessons of Lebanon: Don't Forget to Leave," *The New York Times*, March 30, 2003.

world politics. States that early came into being and early developed a sense of nationhood (as opposed to areas that merely shared a common culture and/or language) were favored in the world arena. States in Eastern Europe, Africa, South Asia, and the Middle East generally have been weaker because many of them did not become independent until the early or mid-twentieth century. Turkey and Iran, which experienced national revolutions early in that century, seemingly enjoy a greater sense of state integrity and stability than many of the Islamic states that became independent after World War I or World War II. Fragile states with weak governance engender problems that can lead to internal and external hostilities and conflicts.

During the Cold War the United States and the United Soviet Socialist Republics (USSR) often confronted each other through surrogates and in struggles taking place in what was then called the "Third World." In fact, it can be argued that the first battle of the Cold War was the US–USSR confrontation over Iran and Azerbaijan in 1946, when, in a sense, the United States assumed the role the British had played earlier in preventing Russian expansion to the south into Persia. US relations in the Islamic world with ally states *vis-à-vis* Soviet client states helped thwart the communist drive for world domination. There are those who argue that the defeat of the USSR in Afghanistan was the critical step to the fall of the Berlin Wall and the ultimate collapse of the Soviet Union. In saying this today one cannot but note the unintended consequences that US support in Afghanistan for the mujahidīn (freedom fighters) from throughout the Islamic world subsequently had in strengthening the militant extremist Islamic movements that had been growing since the 1930s and had burst upon the world's stage with the 1979 Iranian Shi'ite revolution.

The collapse of the Soviet Union, it should be noted, also added to the number of majority Islamic population states. The former republics of the USSR of Kazakhstan, Kyrgyzstan, Tajikistan, Turkmenistan, and

Uzbekistan became independent in Central Asia. Radical Islam has made some inroads in these countries during the 1990s; but its influence remains limited to date in societies that had been greatly secularized under Soviet communism.[39]

The growth of radical Islam has been spurred by the Israeli–Arab wars and Israeli–Palestinian conflicts that began in earnest with the founding of the State of Israel in 1948. The details of the dispute are not the subject of this chapter but the Israeli–Palestinian struggle has been the major nutrient for radical Islam's growth and strength. The conflict will continue to provoke the Islamic world until there is an accepted and legal arrangement by which Israel is secure as a state, the Palestinians have a viable state, and the holy shrines of all three monotheistic religions are acceptably managed and made accessible for believers of all three religions.

The mother of Islamic militant organizations is the Muslim Brotherhood founded in Egypt in the 1930s. It helped to give birth to the Palestinian organizations Hamas and Islamic Jihad, to Lebanon's Hizbullah and to Osama bin Laden's al-Qaeda. The strength of Islamic fundamentalism is in part due to these groups' social services, medical care, and religious education as an alternative to the inadequate support of their populations by failing states. The appeal is not only to the poor but to the entire society and the educated. The force of anti-Western, radical Islam is driven by alienation and anger at politically bankrupt governments of some of the Islamic countries, and by Muslims' conviction that the West, particularly the United States, has not been balanced in its treatment of the Islamic world, especially with respect to the Palestinian–Israeli conflict. Unfortunately, this

---

39 Svante E. Cornell, "The US Redraws the Map," *The Foreign Service Journal*, vol. 80, no. 4, April, 2003, p. 20.

may have caused many Muslims to associate democracy as being anti-Islamic.[40]

Gilles Kepel says that the beginning of the current Islamist radical movement is marked by Egypt's decision in 1966 to execute Sayyed Qutb, a theorist who rejected nationalism and urged the creation of a new Qur'anic generation.[41] At the same time violent acts by secular Palestinian terrorist groups served to identify Muslims with terrorism.[42] The radical Islamist movement became more visible after the 1973 Arab–Israeli war. The decade of the 1970s was capped by the 1979 Iranian revolution.

During the 1980s militant Muslims launched a number of military *jihads*, including taking on the Soviet troops in Afghanistan. Hizbullah in Lebanon fought Israel. Muslim terrorists assassinated President Anwar Sadat of Egypt, and the first Palestinian *Intifada* in 1987 contributed to the rise of Hamas and Islamic Jihad in the Palestinian Authority.

The mujahidīn victory in Afghanistan in 1992 dispersed the battle-toughened fighters to other countries for struggles. Fundamentalist Muslims first bombed the World Trade Center in New York City in 1993; attacked the American liaison mission in Riyadh, Saudi Arabia, in 1995; raided the military living quarters in Khobar, Saudi Arabia in 1996; bombed two US Embassies in East Africa in 1998; attacked the *USS Cole* in a Yemeni port in 2000; and again attacked the Twin Towers in New York City and the Pentagon in Washington, D.C. in 2001. The mujahidīns' experiences in Algeria, Bosnia and Egypt in the 1990s, where they were defeated, is marked by Kepel as the beginning of the movement's

---

40 Youssef Ibrahim, "Spiking the Illusion of Democracy in the Middle East," *The Washington Post Outlook Section*, March 23, 2003, p. B3.

41 Robin Wright, "Mosque and State: A French academic argues that the mulitant Islamic theocracy has run its course," *The New York Times Book Review*, Sunday, May 26, 2002, p. 10 in which Wright reviews Gilles Kepel, *The Trail of Political Islam* (The Belknap Press/Harvard University Press, 2002).

42 Phyllis E. Oakley, chapter 6, "International Terrorism: What Can We Do About It?" in David L. Boren and Edward J. Perkins (eds.), *Democracy, Morality, and the Search for Peace in America's Foreign Policy* (Norman: The University of Oklahoma Press, 2002), pp. 63–64.

decline. This was accompanied by the loss of zeal for the Shi'ite revolution in Iran. He says that between 1995 and 1997, the season of military *jihad* began to end.[43] The mujahidīn attacks on the United States were, in a sense, acts to try to reinvigorate a movement in decline.

Accepting that the religious tenets of Islam are compatible with democracy and peace and that the history of Islamic empires and countries shows them to be generally tolerant and peaceful, and assuming that the radical Islamic movement so threatening in recent decades really is running out of support, the future of the Islamic world could become promising. What is needed is for Muslim countries to move toward more liberal and open societies, for life to become steadily better for all peoples in Islamic countries, and for Israelis and Palestinians to negotiate a lasting settlement of their dispute.

The United States has an important role in promoting progress in all three of these areas. Prince El Hassan has shown clearly that the beliefs and teachings of true Islam are constructive for democracy and world peace. The history of Islam shows the same. Perhaps the fanaticism of the radicals has peaked. We in America must seize the opportunity to use judiciously our wealth, power, and influence in the Islamic world for our own national interests and in the interests of the entire world.

---

43 Robin Wright, *Mosque and State*, p. 10.

Further Reading

This Further Reading section details the major publications of Prince El Hassan, David L. Boren, Edward J. Perkins, and Alain Elkann.

His Royal Highness Prince El Hassan bin Talal

HRH Prince El Hassan bin Talal's Official Website is at
http://www.elhassan.org

The site documents Prince El Hassan's political and personal life, and his valuable role in promoting world peace.

Prince El Hassan is the author of the following books:

A Study on Jerusalem (1979) (English).

Palestinian Self-Determination (1981) (English; Arabic).

Search for Peace (1984) (English; Arabic).

Christianity in the Arab World (1994) (English; Arabic; French; Greek; Spanish; Russian; German).

Continuity, Innovation and Change: Selected Essays (2001).

In Memory of Faisal I: The Iraqi Question (2003) (Arabic).

Q & A: Contemporary Issues (2003) (Arabic).

Essere Musulmano [To Be A Muslim], co-author with Alain Elkann (2001) (Italian, French, and Spanish).

His Royal Highness has been a prolific contributor to newspapers, magazines, periodicals as well as publications on regional and international issues. Details are provided on the website detailed above.

David L. Boren

Preparing America's Foreign Policy for the 21st Century, editor with Edward J. Perkins. Norman, OK: University of Oklahoma Press, 1999.

Democracy, Morality, and the Search for Peace in America's Foreign Policy, editor with Edward J. Perkins. Norman, OK: University of Oklahoma Press, 2002.

"The Winds of Change at the CIA," *Yale Law Journal* 101 (1992): 853.

"The Intelligence Community: How Crucial?" *Foreign Affairs*, vol. 71, no. 3 (1992).

"A Second Chance," *The Washington Post*, March 15, 1991.

"New World, New CIA," *New York Times*, 17 June, 1990, E21.

"Time for a Change in U.S. Intelligence?: World Changes Call for New Structure," *The World & I*, July 1992.

"The World Needs an Army on Call," *New York Times*, August 26, 1992.

"Rethinking US Intelligence," *Defense Intelligence Journal*, vol. 1, no. 1 (Spring 1992).

Edward J. Perkins

Preparing America's Foreign Policy for the 21ˢᵗ Century, editor with David L. Boren. Norman, OK: University of Oklahoma Press, 1999.

Foreword to, *Palestinian Refugees: Old Problems – New Solutions*, edited by Joseph Ginat and Edward J. Perkins. Norman, OK: University of Oklahoma Press; Brighton: Sussex Academic Press, 2001.

Democracy, Morality, and the Search for Peace in America's Foreign Policy, editor with David L. Boren. Norman, OK: University of Oklahoma Press, 2002.

Foreword to *The Middle East Peace Process: Vision versus Reality*, edited by Joseph Ginat, Edward J. Perkins, and Edwin G. Corr. Norman, OK: University of Oklahoma Press; Brighton: Sussex Academic Press, 2002.

"New Dimensions in Foreign Affairs: Public Administration Theory in Practice," *Public Administration Review*, July–August 1990.

"Diversity in U.S. Diplomacy," *The Bureaucrat*, vol. 20, no. 4 (1991–92).

"The United States and the UN," *Yale University Law Journal* (1993).

"The United States as a Global Citizen, " *Presidential Studies Quarterly* (1992).

"Should the United Nations Have a Standing Army?" *The Georgetown Compass – A Journal of International Affairs*, vol. III, no. 2 (Fall 1993).

"Global Institutions: Action for the Future," U.S. Catholic Conference, 1994.

"Resolution of Conflict, the Attainment of Peace," Occasional Paper Number 96/1, University of Sydney, Centre for Peace and Conflict Studies, 1996.

"An International Agenda for Change," *American Behavioral Scientist*, vol. 40, no. 3 (January 1997).

"The Psychology of Diplomacy: Conflict Resolution in a Time of Minimal or Unusual Small-Scale Conflicts." Chapter 4 in *The Psychology of Peacekeeping*, edited by Harvey J. Langholtz. Westport, CT: Praeger, 1998.

Alain Elkann

Alain Elkann is the author of several interviews in book form, including:

Vita di Moravia/A Life of Moravia (Bompiani 1989), translated into fifteen languages.

Cambiare il Cuore / To Change One's Heart (Bompiani, 1993), an interview with Cardinal Carlo Maria Martini, published in France, Spain and Japan.

Essere Ebreo/On Being Jewish (Bompiani, 1994), an interview with Rabbi Elio Toaff.

Index

About the cover illustration

Ismail Hakki Altunbezer was known for his harmonious compositions in *jalī thuluth*. This *levha* is a masterpiece of balance and symmetry. The *alifs* and *lams* are equally spaced within the round field. The two *'ayns*, looped and rounded, fall symmetrically on both sides of the circle, while the *mim* and *ra'* in the middle reflect each other's shape. The recursive *ya'* divides the plate in the middle; the letters ﺘ at the top and the ﺴ in the bottom complete the harmony of the composition as a whole. The letters are positioned so that even without the vowel markers and other calligraphic signs, there is no sense of empty spaces. This wonderful construction was so greatly admired by later calligraphers that they frequently imitated it. Mrs. Riffat Kunt (1321/1903 – 1406/1986) decorated the sides in *halkari* style.